A Disciple's Devotional

Jeff Leis

Author:
Jeff Leis

Art Director & Designers:
Sarah Kohn
Matt Shumaker

Content Editors:
Polly Alterman
Dr. Tino Ballesteros
Sarah Kohn
Matt Shumaker
Becca Whitmyre

Photo Credit:
b.whitmyre Photography

Published by Yosemite Church
© 2016 Jeff Leis
First printing 2016

Printed in the United States of America

Table of Contents

Introduction

Why is this devotional significant for a follower of Christ?

Most of us crave well being. We want our days to go well. For the most part we want to feel valued, special to someone, secure and connected in a meaningful way to others. Psychologist and counselor Larry Crabb files all of these things under two headings: Security and Significance. These basic needs often operate under the radar of our conscience thoughts. When unmet, they create a measure of discomfort and motivate us (often unconsciously) toward behaviors and choices that we believe will either meet those needs or distract us from them.

The Christian life (a disciple's journey) is the process of connecting to God in an ever-deepening way and growing with others in spiritual community so we can experience God meeting those basic needs in the healthiest way possible, this side of Heaven.

Jesus came to introduce us to freedom. Freedom from our sin, from guilt and shame, our obsession with possessions and lust for more – more things, more excitement, more sex, more options. We live in a culture that has brainwashed us to believe that we need 250 TV channels, 24 different flavors of ranch dressing, and as many Facebook friends as possible. Why? Because we have bought into the illusion that we will somehow be worth more if we have more of these things. Our value rises with the number of our valuables. We have been duped into thinking that we'll be more special if we can just get others to think so.

The truth is that none of these things will ever fully satisfy because they were never intended to do so. God wants us to enjoy what we have along with the relationships around us. When I try to build my identity on any entity other than Him, I'll never win. C.S. Lewis said it this way: "God designed the human machine to run on Himself. He Himself is the fuel our spirits were designed to burn, or the food our spirits were designed to feed on. There is no other. That is why it is just no good asking God to make us happy in our own way without bothering about religion. God cannot give us a happiness and peace apart from Himself, because it is not there."

Our freedom comes out of a relationship with Jesus and all that He is. Jesus told us that He is the truth and would set us free if we held to His teaching. He is the light who could help us to see out of our darkness; He is the way that can lead us to life and life eternal. Those that choose His way are called disciples. Dallas Willard reminds us: "The New Testament was written by disciples, about disciples, for disciples."

This devotional will empower you to know and experience your identity at a deeper level, one that can only be found in a transformational relationship with Christ.

Who has this devotional been written for?

This is *A Disciple's Devotional*. It was written so the beautiful collection of believers and seekers that attend Yosemite Church, those I am blessed to serve, can make clear and marked movement into the very best that God has for them. Jesus does not call us to a floundering faith, but one that should and can flourish. He does not invite us into an insecure identity but rather one that, when developed properly, creates a deep and genuine confidence that flows out of His indwelling presence. Jesus wasn't vague about how to find our true value and purpose, yet many believers struggle to experience the significance that flows freely from a life dedicated to Him.

One does not have to belong to Yosemite Church to take this journey. All you need is the desire to know who God has made you to be, and how to strengthen your new identity in Him.

How to get the most from this devotional?

The principles woven into this 40-day adventure are designed to help create the foundation that every Christ-follower needs to sustain a growing and vibrant faith – one that's clearly evident to others and generates the kind of influence that Jesus said would mark and define those who know Him. You will not benefit as much from this devotional if you complete it in isolation. It will have its best impact as you invite others to participate with you. It is a 40-day devotional designed to be completed over eight weeks. Each week is formatted so you can have 5 days on and two days off. At the break of each week, there is set of questions to process with others.

There is a reason many believers struggle with an anemic faith – they have never been discipled. They enter into a relationship with Christ (uttered a prayer to accept Him) but have never been trained to obey His commands (so they will become like Him). They attend church with a measure of regularity but are very irregular in spending personal time with Jesus. They have settled for attending the large gathering of believers on the weekend to the neglect of growing in intimate community throughout their week. This devotional is intended (when done with sincerity and within community) to break the habits that produce a shallow, ineffective faith and replace them with spiritual disciplines that cultivate a deeper experience of Christ's presence and purpose that will take you uncharted and glorious places.

Week 1

Our first week will open up our time by defining three Biblical terms that run deep in the Scriptures and in the lives of believers who are learning to follow closely the lifestyle and commands of Christ.

Then we'll examine seven characteristics that I picked up from Willow Creek Community Church. I have discovered these areas to be critical for those wanting to do ministry over the long haul.

Lastly, we'll examine two lists of motivations that can either kill or build a sustainable faith.

Orientation & Introduction

I'm glad you are serious about your role as a disciple. It is crucial that we align ourselves to what God has revealed about discipleship and how it should impact our core identity. As you spend the next two months evaluating your commitment and calling, I pray that you will consciously examine this carefully prepared material. Each day is designed to give you a clearer picture of some aspect of a disciple's journey toward spiritual maturity. The effectiveness of the local church will be determined by how well each of us is growing and becoming the person Christ wants us to be as members of His body. The great evangelist, John Wesley, said: "Without God, we cannot. Without us, He will not."

The journey of discipleship was never intended to be done in isolation. Discipleship is the pursuit of becoming like Christ. Conviction follows our conversion. When we are in relationship with Christ, we no longer live life independent of God. Instead, we accept our dependence upon God and an independance on the body of Christ, within which He calls us to be an active participant.

As you work through *A Disciple's Devotional*, I will use several terms to describe the kind of person Christ calls each of us to be. Each of these Scriptural terms refer to those who follow and commit themselves to Christ.

The first term is "**Disciple**." This is the most prominent term used in the New Testament to identify Christ followers. The word "Disciple" is used 269 times. The word "Christian," in contrast, is used only 3 times and is always referring to the disciples. Dallas Willard says: "The New Testament was written about disciples, by disciples, for disciples."

The second term is "**Member**," or "Membership." This is the term the Bible uses to describe those who have committed themselves to being part of the local church family, or the body of Christ.

What I like about the term "Member" is the implication of belonging with others within the body of Christ. One of the first passages we will study this week will explain why this term fits so well as a description of those who have "joined" or "committed themselves" to cooperate with God's people for God's work.

The final term is "**Servant**," or "Servant-hood." There is probably no better term to describe how Christ lived, and how He calls every disciple to live. Servanthood stands out as the chief attribute of all Christ followers regardless of their giftedness or function in ministry. As disciples, we are active participants in the ministry of the church, and called to model a life of servanthood.

How to Use this Devotional

You will need your Bible to accompany this study. The material is divided into 40 days and takes 20-30 minutes daily to prayerfully work through, so please prioritize adequate time. I suggest you set aside Monday through Friday, and use your weekend days to "catch-up" if you need it. Please do not try to cram multiple days into one.

The more you prioritize your time to work daily on this devotional, the more you will form a healthy habit of study and connection to Christ and the word of God.

Be sure to dialogue with a leader, coach, accountability partner, or mentor any questions that arise out of the study. At the end of each week, you will find a section titled, "Your Week in Review." Use this section to facilitate a time of reflection and dialogue. Please be prepared to share what you have learned about discipleship (your connection to Christ), membership (your growing relationship with other believers), and servanthood.

Yours in Christ,
Pastor Jeff

Preparation Time

To make the most of this devotional, find a quiet place to work through each day's material. Psalm 46:10 reminds us: *"Be still, and know that I am God."* Once you have quieted yourself, take a few minutes and prayerfully consider the following:

– Are there attitudes or perspectives I need to submit to Christ's Lordship in my life?

– Are there areas of sin that I need to confess?

– After you have surrendered the above areas, ask the Lord to reveal His purposes for your life through this study.

Before you finish today, write your first gut reaction toward each of the key terms below, i.e., scared, excited, intimidated, etc.

1) Disciple:

2) Member:

3) Servant:

For the remainder of this week, we will look at seven crucial qualities for spiritual development. Jesus is the portrait of servanthood. He illustrates a life driven by service, not status, and by humility instead of a hunger for power.

As you examine these seven qualities, you might feel like your life reflects a less than perfect match. That's okay so long as your heart desires to pursue them.

Allow the Lord to draw you into a more focused pursuit to be His servant/disciple. Today we look at the first two of the seven qualities: 1) Being a "Christ Follower"; and 2) Your "Character."

Christ Follower – Disciples Have a Passion For Christ

Christ is the single most distinguishing factor from all other religious systems. Jesus makes all the difference. His life is the one we want to emulate. His words are the transcript of our faith. His death and resurrection are the greatest apologetic to our beliefs. C.S. Lewis said: "I believe in Christianity as I believe the sun has risen: not only because I see it, but because by it I see everything else."

Today, the most predominant characteristic of a disciple is being a "Christ follower." Jesus' words to the early disciples left no doubt in their minds. *"Come, follow me…"* (Mark 1:17), was a clear invitation to make Jesus the guiding light of their lives. After looking up the passages below, answer each corresponding question about how you are learning to follow Christ.

—Turning from sin in my life to following Christ (1 Jn 1:9; Ro 6:6)

☐ Poor   ☐ Fair   ☐ Good   ☐ Excellent

– Spending time in God's Word, and in prayer to know Christ better (Cl 3:16; 1 Pe 2:2)

☐ Poor   ☐ Fair   ☐ Good   ☐ Excellent

– Being filled with His Spirit – learning to give Him control of my life (Ro 12:3; Ga 5:16-18, 22-25; Ep 5:18)

☐ Poor   ☐ Fair   ☐ Good   ☐ Excellent

– Using my gifts in ministry as an expression of my passion to follow His example of service (Ro 12:3-8; 1 Pe 4:10-11)

☐ Poor   ☐ Fair   ☐ Good   ☐ Excellent

– Learning to persevere in adversity, and trusting Him to work all things for good (Ro 5:3-5; Ph 1:29; 1 Pe 4:12-14)

☐ Poor   ☐ Fair   ☐ Good   ☐ Excellent

Character – Disciples Pay Attention To The Heart

Depth of character is a matter of becoming more like Christ and less like the world. Oswald Chambers, beloved author of *My Utmost For His Highest*, said: "God can give us a pure heart in an instant, but He cannot quickly bring us Christian character. That takes time and can come only through a series of right moral choices."

Don't be discouraged, my friend, if your character development is not where you want it to be. The more critical question is not where you are now, but where is your character headed? What area in your life and character has God been transforming?

1 Timothy 1:5 says: *"The goal of this command is love which comes from a pure heart and a good conscience and a sincere faith."*

What do you think Paul means when he tells Timothy that our goal/target is "love?" To hit the target or goal, Paul says three things are necessary: a pure heart, good conscience and a sincere faith. How do you maintain these in your life?

Prayer Focus:
I have written a prayer focus for each day. I encourage you simply to engage the Lord in prayer, a conversation between you and your Savior, your Friend, the One you are learning to follow. Use my Prayer Focus, create your own, or make it a combination. I want to help you establish a habit of submitting everything you learn to Him in prayer.

"Lord, I want to be a better follower. Help me to know You more, so that more of who I am will reflect who You are. Amen."

DAY 2
Calling & Commitmet

Calling & Commitment

Disciples Are Called to Care About People

Disciples have a heart for others. They see others with compassion, as Christ saw them in Matthew 9:36-38:

"When he saw the crowds, he had compassion on them, because they were harassed and helpless, like sheep without a shepherd. Then he said to his disciples, "The harvest is plentiful, but the workers are few. Ask the Lord of the harvest, therefore, to send out workers into his harvest field."

How has God impressed upon you the call for compassion, or the conviction to use what you have for the care of others? The size of the need – "the harvest" – is what Jesus says should compel us to be a part of the solution. That is the call. Jesus is asking: "Will you help?" Mother Teresa said: "When I look at the masses, I'll never act. When I look at the one, I will." How are you doing at answering His call to care about others? Would you say you have a high or low level of compassion for others and why?

Disciples Are Called To Grow in their Competence

Disciples are willing to assume responsibility for a task. They take time to develop life skills needed to participate effectively in service and community. Disciples also possess the ability to have some area of ministry "turned over" to them (Ac 6:3). As you read through the following list, check areas where you feel most or least competent:

Most Least

☐	☐	Time management
☐	☐	Conflict resolution
☐	☐	Effective listening skills
☐	☐	Able to explain, in an easy way, the Big God story & how to commit to Christ
☐	☐	Know how to help new belivers develop a strong faith
☐	☐	Able to recognize and respond appropriately to your personal issue (ways you act out in the flesh)
☐	☐	Understand your spiritual gifts and are using them as a part of Christ's church/body
☐	☐	Know how to have a daily time to connect authentically with Jesus and do so consistently

Over the upcoming weeks, we will look closely at the areas of development and how to build greater competency.

Commitment- Disciples Do What It Takes

Servant-hood requires commitment, not convenience. We will never advance God's kingdom because it is easy or convenient. It will only happen as we take measures to draw upon Him for the strength to keep our commitments. Disciples are devoted to personal growth, to see others grow in Christ, and to reach other people for Christ. How do the following passages call us to reach others?
Matthew 28:18-20; Romans 16:1-4; 2 Timothy 2:2.

Do you see yourself as a "servant" or "minister" of Christ? If so, how have you been stretched in your dedication to ministry? Has God dealt with any attitude of "convenience" that has challenged you to be more committed? If so, please describe.

Prayer Focus:
Harry Emerson Fosdick, a Presbyterian pastor from the last century said: "No life ever grows great until it is focused, dedicated and disciplined." Ask the Lord to help you to grow a great life. Spend a few minutes praying for your focus, dedication and discipline.

"Lord, use me to be a blessing to others within the body of Christ, and help me to choose not to serve just because I might not be 'good enough.' Help me, Lord, to get better at the things that matter most. Amen."

Cooperation & Capacity

Disciples Cooperate With Leaders and Those They Serve

Today, we look at your ability to cooperate with others and your capacity as a disciple. Being a disciple requires making room for ministry and doing whatever it takes to make your contribution. This means prioritizing time, energy, and resources for service. Servants must have the capacity (spiritual, emotional and physical resources) to do what God has called them to do.

Serving in ministry requires cooperation with those in leadership, and with those with whom we serve. Teams are successful when people with different gifts and skills work together. Disciples are called to serve and be participants. What do the following passages tell us about partnering and cooperating with others to create a stronger team/church body? As you read 1 Corinthians 12 and Romans 12:4-8, make note of how the word "part" is used.

Write what you observed from the above passages.

What do you believe makes an effective team?

What part of Christ's body do you think you are?

Discipleship Requires A Capacity To Serve

Capacity. This important area is often overlooked. Some individuals may have the other six qualities (Christ follower, character, calling, competence, cooperation and even commitment) and yet have a plate so full, they are unable to serve. Steven Pauls said: "The space for what you want has already been filled with what you have settled for instead." Peter Drucker said: "We must know the value of planned abandonment; we must decide what not to do."

What do the following passages ask its original reader to "give up?" (Mt 8:21-22, 16:24-26; Ph 2:3)

To what have you said "no", so that you can say "yes" to ministry? Describe the experience.

Is there something you need to give up, so that you can say "yes" to ministry?

Prayer Focus:
"Planned abandonment" is not an easy task. When we realize that there is something better we can be doing, we have better clarity. God wants to give us a life of peace, joy, mercy, community, friendship and fulfillment; but until we are ready to make space for Him and for His kingdom, we will continue to hold on to things and activities that just make us stressed and tired. Tell the Lord today what you want to release, so you can get a better grip on Him and His kingdom.

Motivation

In Luke 6:45 Jesus said:
"The good man brings good things out of the good stored up in his heart, and the evil man brings evil things out of the evil stored up in his heart. For out of the overflow of his heart his mouth speaks."

Zig Ziglar said:
"People often say that motivation doesn't last. Well, neither does bathing – that's why we recommend it daily."

Today we look at two lists. One focuses on "healthy" motives, and the other "unhealthy" motives for service. As you do so, remember that no one operates with 100% purity all of the time. Serving in ministry requires constant development. Psalm 51:6 (MSG) says: *"What you're after is truth from the inside out. Enter me, then; conceive a new, true life."* Each day requires an intentional focus on the best that is within us.

Healthy Motives
Under each of the following passages, explain how you can apply it to your own life.

Glorify (honor) the Lord
"Whatever you do, work at it with all your heart, as working for the Lord, not for men, since you know that you will receive an inheritance from the Lord as a reward. It is the Lord Christ you are serving."
Colossians 3:23-24

Bear Fruit in your Life
"This is to my Father's glory, that you bear much fruit, showing yourselves to be my disciples."
John 15:8

Use your Gifts to Serve One Another
"Each one should use whatever gifts he has recieved to serve others, faithfully administering God's grace in its various forms."
1 Peter 4:10

Be Gracious to those who Fail
"... God was reconciling the world to himself in Christ, not counting men's sins against them. And he has committed to us the message of reconciliation. We are therefore Christ's ambassadors, as though God were making his appeal through us." 2 Corinthians 5:19-20

Prayer Focus:
As you close your time, please remember to lift up in prayer anyone you know who is currently going through this material. Pray specifically that our church Council, elders and staff will have wisdom and be protected and strengthened as they lead. Pray for your leader or coach, and ask God to knit your hearts together as you learn from one another.

Ask the Lord to show you any motivations that need adjustment.

Wrong Motives & Hindrance to Service

Wrong or unhealthy motives are a part of our "flesh." Everyone has wrong motives, but only those willing to face them can change them. The following phrases are either a wrong motive or the behaviour that can surface out of a wrong or distorted motivation.

See if you can identify any of the following areas as places where you may be vulnerable. How does it manifest itself in your life?

Self-Exaltation
"Let another praise you, and not your own mouth; someone else, and not your own lips."
Proverbs 27:2

To Feel Important or Gain Prestige
"We speak as men approved by God to be entrusted with the gospel. We are not trying to please men but God, who tests our hearts. You know we never used flattery, nor did we put on a mask to cover up greed – God is our witness. We were not looking for praise from men, not from you or anyone else." 1 Thessalonians 2:4-6

Having a Short Fuse or Exhibiting Outbursts of Anger

James tells us that the anger of man does not achieve the righteousness of God (Ja 1:19-20). God's work is accomplished by one who listens attentively, speaks only when necessary, and is slow to anger. We need to manage our anger appropriately. (Ga 5:19-20; Ep 4:31; Cl 3:8).

Unconfessed Sin

We are called to confess our sins. John says: *"If we confess our sins, he is faithful and just and will forgive us our sins and purify us from all unrighteousness"* (1 Jn 1:9). Any sin that has control of us (Ro 6:16) must be confessed and brought under the lordship of Christ (Ac 2:38). If there is any unaddressed sin, it can stagnate our growth, or even derail our progress.

After reading this section, how would you say you've learned to deal with personal wrong motives, or hindrances to your life with Christ? Sometimes through failure, God gives us greater insight into areas that need attention. Usually, it is then that our willingness to learn and surrender is the greatest. Describe a time when you had to make a "heart" or attitude adjustment.

Prayer Focus:
Look over each of the potential "Wrong Motives" and write a prayer that submits that area of vulnerability to Christ. Ask the Lord to reveal to your heart when any of these motivational distractions might be rising within you.

Week In Review Questions

1. On Day 1, Pastor Jeff introduced three key terms that are prominent throughout this study. What were your first "gut reactions" to each word/term? How are these terms or concepts similar and how are they different?

2. From Day 1 to Day 3, we looked at seven areas of development: Christ Follower, Character, Calling, Competence, Cooperation, Commitment and Capacity. Which area spoke to you the most and why?

3. Look specifically at your observations from Day 2, under "called to grow in their competence." Where were you the most competent, and why?

4. On Day 4 and Day 5, we looked at right and wrong motives. All of us are guilty from time to time of having wrong motives. To which wrong motive did you feel most vulnerable and why?

5. Were there any other insights or discoveries from this week that you would like to share?

After sharing your answers with your accountability partner, mentor, leader or small group, take a few minutes to pray for one another. If you are new to public prayer, just try to pray one sentence, like this: "Lord, thank you for _____, their friendship and acceptance. Amen."

This week, we focus each day on one of our five values. An organization's values are its guiding principles, non-negotiables that ring true regardless of cultural fluctuation. Our YC values were articulated several years ago and are easy to remember. In order for our values to have a significant impact on our church, we must embrace them and communicate them at every level of our church's structure and life. This week we ask ourselves how we personally express the values of our church.

Inspired Word

Find that quiet place again, then reflect on the value for the day. Answer a few questions of personal application and then copy the "memory verse" for that value onto a 3x5 card for the purpose of committing it to memory. You cannot do what you cannot remember. By memorizing each key verse and value, you will begin to build a stronger connection to God's Word.

As you read the Scripture and comment, try to guess the corresponding "I.W." words for that value. As you close your time, remember to pray for those in leadership, asking that God will protect and keep them focused on Him.

1. We value the _____
of God.

Memory Verse:
"All Scripture is God-breathed and is useful for teaching, rebuking, correcting and training in righteousness, so that the man of God may be thoroughly equipped for every good work." 2 Timothy 3:16-17

After reading the Scripture, can you guess the value that it represents? The "Inspired Word," (the answer to #1) the Bible, is not just a book; it is a living expression of God, revealing Himself to mankind.
Read Hebrews 4:12-13 and answer this question:
How do you practically seek to let the Scriptures serve as your personal authority?

Read 2 Timothy 2:15. What do you think the author is challenging us to do or be, and how does this Scripture fit into that?

"Do your best to present yourself to God as one approved, a workman who does not need to be ashamed and who correctly handles the word of truth." 2 Timothy 2:15

A young believer was discouraged in his attempts to read and remember the Bible. He said: "It's no use. No matter how much I read, I always forget what I have just read." His pastor gave him this perspective, "When you pour water over a sieve, no matter how much you pour, you don't collect much water. But you do end up having a clean sieve."

I'd like to suggest a couple of thoughts to help you raise the value of the Inspired Word of God in your own life.

Getting into the Word:

1) So what's important is not you getting through the Bible but that the Bible gets through you. If you never put the Scriptures in, God has nothing to bring out. We utilize a reading schedule that will take you through the Bible in one year – that's you getting through the Bible. Using a Journal and the tool of the acrostic below to hear and know God better – that's the Bible getting through you. Here's how it works. Each day you read, open your Journal and respond to the SOAP acrostic by writing:

S = Scripture for that day

O = Observation from the text

A = a personal Application from the text that you can apply directly to your life

P = is what you will Pray about; or better, your written prayer stimulated by your reading and study.

Getting the Word into you:

2) Conviction is worthless unless it is converted into conduct. I might be inspired to read and know the Scriptures, to articulate what I believe; but until meditation of truth is woven into the fabric of my life, I'll never achieve the spiritual life to which God is calling me. If you can consistently dedicate 5-15 minutes of the best part of your day (when you are the most alert and sharp) and fill it with God's truth, I guarantee you will experience a magnificent change in your choices and behavior. As we move forward as a church, it is crucial that we, as the individual members, live out our value of the Inspired Word of God.

On the next page do your own SOAP entry on our memory verse for this Value, 2 Timothy 3:16.

Your SOAP:

_____

_____

_____

_____

_____

_____

_____

_____

_____

_____

_____

_____

_____

_____

_____

_____

_____

_____

_____

_____

Prayer Focus:
I'd like to introduce you to a concept called "pray the Scriptures." The idea is to take a given passage and simply put the text into a prayer. This week as you close each day, try to pray through the memory verse for that day. Today's prayer might go something like this:

"Lord, all Scripture is breathed out by you. As I read and meditate on your word, teach me what I need to know. Redirect me if I am falling away from you. Correct me if I am straying from the path, and train me to stay the course, so that I will become thoroughly equipped for every good work. Amen."

Day 7
Five Values

Intrinsic Worth

As you examine our second value, I trust you will be comforted and encouraged by what you learn. Today's value fits nicely with a quote from St. Augustine, one of our earliest Church fathers (300 A.D.): "God loves each of us as if there were only one of us."

2. We value the _____
 of every person
(the "I.W." answer is below the verses for this value).

"So God created man in his own image, in the image of God he created him; male and female he created them." Genesis 1:27

"For God so loved the world that he gave his one and only Son, that whoever believes in him shall not perish but have eternal life." John 3:16

Memory Verse:
"For you created my inmost being; you knit me together in my mother's womb. I praise you because I am fearfully and wonderfully made; your works are wonderful, I know that full well." Psalms 139:13-14

"Intrinsic Worth" (the answer to #2) are the "I.W." words for this value. Because each person is made in God's own image and because each one is valuable enough for God to sacrifice His son for us, each of us has eternal value, Intrinsic Worth.

How can this value impact the way you see and treat others?

What implication do you see for our church because of this value?

It's normal to wonder if anyone would ever notice our absence. We can feel insignificant in such a busy world.

Sir Michael Costa once conducted a rehearsal in which the orchestra was joined by a great chorus. About half-way through the session, with trumpets blaring, drums rolling, and violins singing their rich melody, the piccolo player muttered to himself: "What good am I doing? I might as well not be playing. Nobody can hear me." So he placed his instrument to his lips but did not engage it with his breath. Within moments the conductor cried out: "Stop! Stop! Where is the piccolo?"

I'm sure that many who were in attendance did not realize the piccolo was missing, but the most important person did. Why? Because his ears were trained to hear each instrument. He had developed an awareness of what was essential to communicate the heart of the musical expression.

When we value the Intrinsic Worth of people, we seek to develop an ear to the sound of people who feel insignificant, who question if anyone would notice them, or miss them when they are gone.

We can effectively love people as we build relationships where others are welcomed into a place to be heard, listened to, valued and cared for. You can't hear everyone, but you can hear someone. Maybe your phone call, your encouragement, your interest in their presence or absence would draw them back into the music of God's purposes.

Prayer Focus:
Look back over today's Scriptures. Praying through Scripture is a great way to apply it directly to your heart. For example, Psalm 139:13-14 might sound like this as a prayer:

"Lord, thank you for creating me, for knowing me before I knew myself. Lord, you know me better than I know myself. Even when I doubt my worth and value, I am comforted by the truth that you see me as wonderfully made. Amen."

Let the truth of God's knowledge and purposes for you find a new home in the center of your heart.

Intimate Walk

Today's value is at the heart of all we do. Remember to write out each memory verse on a 3x5 card (or pick up a megapack) to carry it with you as you work to prioritize what we value.

3. We value an _____
 with God
(the "I.W." answer is below the verses for this value).

"Everyone who confesses that Jesus is God's Son participates continuously in an intimate relationship with God." 1 John 4:15 (MSG)

"What you're after is truth from the inside out. Enter me, then; conceive a new, true life." Psalm 51:6 (MSG)

Memory Verse:
"I have told you this so that my joy may be in you and that your joy may be complete. My command is this: Love each other as I have loved you. Greater love has no one than this, that he lay down his life for his friends. You are my friends if you do what I command." John 15:11-14

An "Intimate Walk" with God is at the center of our values. The first two values flow into this value and the last two values flow out of it. From the Scriptures, what do you see and how would you describe this value in your own words?

What have you recently experienced from your intimacy with God?

As the third of five, it is the middle and center of the other four YC Values. When we help people discover intimacy with God, we hit the bullseye.

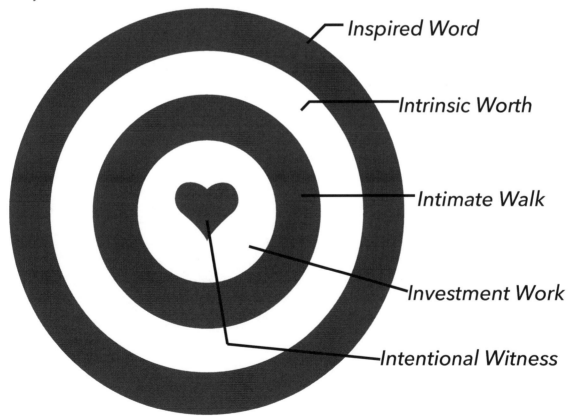

Inspired Word

Intrinsic Worth

Intimate Walk

Investment Work

Intentional Witness

A four-year-old girl ran to her mother with a look of consternation. Hugging a small doll with her pudgy little arms, she said: "Mama, I love her and love her, but she never loves back!"

God loves us with the hope that we would love Him back. We, like the four-year-old girl's doll, often remain unresponsive to God's embrace – not because we are incapable of loving but because we are preoccupied with other things.

Ephesians 5:1-2 says: *"...as dearly loved children ... live a life of love..."* God doesn't want to have a loving encounter with us. He wants a loving relationship. Intimacy must be an ongoing target. Unfortunately, in our busy culture, it can often seem to be a moving target.

When the Psalmist wrote: *"Be still, and know that I am God ..."*, in Psalm 46:10, he wasn't thinking of aiming at a target, but he was aiming (zeroing in on) a more accurate relationship with God.

What are three things that you can do to foster your intimacy with God?

•

•

•

Prayer Focus:
Ask the Lord to remind you what the bullseye value can do for you as you go through each day. Ask Him to show you how you would make wiser choices if you could keep His love in mind.

"Lord, as we seek to walk in intimacy with you, help us to remember that holding still and clearly focusing on our relationship with you is the best way to hit the bullseye – every time."

Investment Work

As a young adult, I worked for The Master's Touch, a small furniture refinishing shop in Gresham, Oregon. I came to the business with some experience. I had refinished antique furniture for my family's antique store for years. My new boss was extremely pleased that he could turn me loose on several projects with very little supervision.

It wasn't long though before both he and I knew where I needed considerable improvement and coaching – the finishing booth. I had never used a spray gun and had never known all that could be accomplished with shading to manipulate the final look of a product.

Over and over, my mentor would show me how to mix, shade, tint, and spray different applications. I loved the chance to improve my part-time trade, and found myself watching his seasoned discernment in multiple areas.

Two things were crucial for my growth as a finisher in those four years at The Master's Touch: 1) I had to remain teachable; and 2) I needed someone who was willing and persistent (and often patient) to teach me. Likewise, in your spiritual journey, you need the Master's touch. Our Master, Jesus, has devised a plan, a mission, and a means by which He wants to develop and improve your ability to love and lead others into a loving relationship with God.

Most of us come to God like the furniture that came to me at The Master's Touch – scratched up, worn down, and sometimes broken. We cannot heal ourselves. We do not experience the mending and rebuilding that God desires without the time and attention and loving patience of someone willing to instruct and guide us in our journey.

Our church will accomplish God's calling as we prioritize our time to invest in discipling relationships. When we do, we will powerfully experience the Master's touch.

Today's value is the driving force behind this Devotional and the work to which it calls us.

4. We value the _____
  of discipleship.

Memory Verse:
"Therefore go and make disciples of all nations, baptizing them in the name of the Father and of the Son and of the Holy Spirit, and teaching them to obey everything I have commanded you. And surely I am with you always, to the very end of the age." Matthew 28:19-20

"Investment Work" (the answer to #4) is our description of the Great Commission. No other Scripture captures the essence of Jesus' assignment. In a single sentence, it is the clearest instruction of what we are to be about.

How would you like to see this value expressed in your life?

How do you think "discipling" would be an investment?

Have you ever been "discipled" by anyone? If so, describe the experience.

Prayer Focus:
As you pray through Matthew 28:19-20, start your prayer by saying:

"Lord, help me to learn to invest in the Great Commission to go and make disciples . . . Lord, show each of us what our next step should be to make this value a personal reality."

Intentional Witness

5. We value the _____ of unity.
(The "I.W." answer is below the verses for this value.)

Memory Verse:
"... I pray also for those who will believe in me through their message, that all of them may be one, Father, just as you are in me and I am in you. May they also be in us so that the world may believe that you have sent me." John 17:20-21

"Make every effort to keep the unity of the Spirit through the bond of peace." Ephesians 4:3

After reading the above Scriptures, what words do you think we've chosen to describe this value? Jesus prays for our unity; He commands our unity, and even tells us why it is of such importance, *"… so that the world may believe that you have sent me."* (Jn 17:21) We must be very intentional about our "witness" of unity; it's not just going to happen. Therefore, "Intentional Witness" (the answer to #5) is our last core value.

What do you think are the barriers to unity in the body of Christ?

How could our church communicate this value?

As individuals, how can we promote unity among believers?

The tactical saying, "divide and conquer," is one of Satan's primary approaches to nullify the effectiveness of any group of believers. It could be a cluster of Christians in the marketplace, a Christian couple or family, or a local church. When The Deceiver can tempt us to be more concerned with our opinion, idea, or agenda than we are with unity, cooperation, and concern for others, he has been successful.

Jesus prayed for the "Intentional Witness of Unity." In John 17:20, He said: "… I pray also for those who will believe in me…" Notice His future tense. He is praying for us, all of the Christ followers, who would join the family of God after His resurrection. He goes on to say in verse 21, "… that all of them may be one, Father, just as you are in me and I am in you. May they also be in us…" Okay, here is where it gets very "Intentional." What happens when we express "oneness?" He finishes verse 21 "… so that the world may believe that you have sent me." WOW! When we illustrate the ability and commitment to **build up** rather than **tear down**, we magnify an unbeliever's exposure to Christ, and we take away a primary obstacle to faith.

Nothing disheartens children more than parents who cannot resolve their past differences. When siblings witness the two most important people in their world embroiled in divorce, or arguing without commitment to reconcile, it compromises their core belief system. In a similar manner, believers send a compromising message to those wondering how a spiritual family could be a viable alternative to the world's system when we fail to *"make every effort to keep the unity of the Spirit through the bond of peace."* Ephesians 4:3

What can you do this week, even today to express the Intentional Witness of unity?

Prayer Focus
"Lord, today we will rub shoulders with believers and unbelievers. We ask for Your power and presence to be seen in us. Lord, inspire in us an intentional (choosing to act) demonstration of our commitment to *"… Love one another…"* (Jn 13:34), as You have loved us. Thank you Lord for our spiritual family. Draw others to Yourself through our relationships. Amen."

Week In Review Questions

1. Have you ever taken the time to articulate your values? Why would such an exercise be meaningful, and what would you choose as your top three values?

2. What is the evidence in a person's life that points to their values?

3. The five values we have looked at this week are in their order for a reason. They build on one another and have a natural movement to them. Why is the "Inspired Word of God" our first value? How is this value being lived out in our church and in your life?

4. What is the significance of the "Intrinsic Worth of Every Person?" How can this value be cultivated in your life as an individual, and as a community of believers?

5. What is the point of the "bullseye" value, and how do you nurture this value in your own life? How would you like to see it nurtured more?

6. We will be talking a lot about discipleship in the weeks to come. What does the wording around this value infer, and how prominent should it be to each of us and why?

7. Concerning our 5th value, how does John 17 impact you, and what you can do to respond more effectively to Jesus' prayer?

Week 3

This week we will continue to focus on our "Core Statements"; our Mission, Vision and Strategy. These are the guiding statements that remind us of our purpose-why we are here, our vision-what that looks like, and begin to unpack our strategy–how we will live out that purpose.

The YC Mission

"Meeting People Where They Are and Loving Them To Where Christ Wants Them To Be."

The well-respected consultant, Peter Drucker, said: "Mission comes first. The mission of nonprofits, including churches, is changed lives." How very accurate he is! We must be about the business of helping people change in order to become more like Christ.

Today, we meditate on our Mission Statement. Meditation and memorization are two of the most powerful tools for a growing believer. Let's ask God to work His calling into our lives. As you read the Scriptures, consider your personal role as a disciple, and try to envision how you can personally contribute to the accomplishment of our mission.

Our Mission
Our Mission is to "Meet people where they are and love them to where Christ wants them to be." We cannot accomplish together what we do not embrace individually. Look up the passages below and describe how you believe Jesus modeled our Mission Statement.

John 3:1-21: The religious teacher, Nicodemus

John 4:4-42: The Samaritan woman

John 8:1-11: The woman caught in adultery

Describe how the following verses connect to our Mission Statement:

"A new command I give you: Love one another. As I have loved you, so you must love one another. By this all men will know that you are my disciples, if you love one another." John 13:34-35

"You have heard that it was said, 'Love your neighbor and hate your enemy.' But I tell you: Love your enemies and pray for those who persecute you, that you may be sons of your Father in heaven. He causes his sun to rise on the evil and the good, and sends rain on the righteous and the unrighteous. If you love those who love you, what reward will you get? Are not even the tax collectors doing that? And if you greet only your brothers, what are you doing more than others? Do not even pagans do that?" Matthew 5:43-47

"Brothers, if someone is caught in a sin, you who are spiritual should restore him gently. But watch yourself, or you also may be tempted. Carry each other's burdens, and in this way you will fulfill the law of Christ." Galatians 6:1-2

How has our study today affected your perspective of our church, and your personal commitment to our mission?

Prayer Focus:
Are you praying for the people around you? Ask the Lord to guide you to those that you can love more effectively. Ask God to help you be intentional about these relationships.

The following prayer comes from Ephesians 1:17-18. Pray this prayer specifically for the relationships God has placed on your heart:

"I keep asking that the God of our Lord Jesus Christ, our glorious Father, may you give _____ the spirit of wisdom and revelation, so that _____ may know Him better. I pray also that the eyes of _____'s heart may be enlightened in order that _____ may know the hope to which He has called them. Amen"

Watch these relationships closely, and continue to ask yourself how you can be a part of God's purposes in their lives.

The YC Vision

Definition of a vision: A picture on the screen of your mind that compels you to move forward despite obstacles

"Where there is no vision, the people perish." Proverbs 29:18 (KJV)

While visiting my parents' home during a holiday, I was amazed at the tireless work my mother put into family photo albums. Close to a dozen albums grace coffee tables and shelves. Each one reflects the value my mother places on family and heritage. Relatives, neighbors and friends sit around for hours perusing the web of connections, hearing stories that complement each photo.

I do not personally believe that "every picture is worth a thousand words." In fact, in the wrong person's hands , the film may not be worth the price to develop it! My son has taken some doozies. What do you do with multiple pictures of one's ceiling, a person's head being left out of the picture, or a photo of your dog's nostril from five inches away? On the other hand, some pictures are "priceless."

I believe pictures fill a need. I know that's a pretty strong statement, but I think it's true. Pictures communicate. They reveal valuable things that can easily be forgotten or overlooked. They remind us of past experiences that hold significance, and they capture how someone or something looks.

Ralph Waldo Emerson said: "Man's actions are the picture book of his creeds." Every life paints a picture. For some of us, we are still very much in the process of development. Others are already over-exposed, and still others feel as if their image has been damaged because of the negatives in their life. What do others see in your actions? Every choice we make puts color and definition on our canvas of life. Our challenge is to have a vision of what we want; or better yet, what God wants others to see in us.

I do not think we should be preoccupied by what others think of us. Rather, we need to be preoccupied by what God thinks of us and who He has called us to be. Jesus said: *"A new command I give you: Love one another. As I have loved you, so you must love one another. By this all men will know that you are my disciples, if you love one another."* John 13:34-35

Would anyone be convinced about the love of God by your love for others? Our Vision Statement is a written description of what we believe it would look like if we, as a community of faith, are so filled up and overtaken by the love God has for us, that we more and more naturally, love God and others as we are called to do.

We are a loving community of growing disciples mentoring the next generation to live the mission of Jesus through the power of the Gospel.

We have been driving our vision into the hearts of our church family for several years now. Until the Vision becomes your personal goal, it remains only a lofty concept. Someone has said: "Vision without action and goals is just an hallucination." Look at the Vision and each of its five main components, then rate yourself on a scale from 1-5 as to your personal understanding and commitment to each of the five areas (1=weakest & 5=strongest).

1 2 3 4 5   I am loved

1 2 3 4 5   I am loving

1 2 3 4 5   I am a disciple

1 2 3 4 5   I am a mentor

1 2 3 4 5   I am a missionary

Now write a short statement explaining your ratings.

Our Vision statement and the subsequent "I am" statements express how Scripture defines believers and their connection to Christ and His mission for the Church. One of the most central issues in every life is the question of personal identity. Over the next couple of weeks, you will study our strategy for helping every person engage in the "cycle of spiritual life/growth." As you go through each day, it is my prayer that you will see how critical it is to have a strategy – a plan for spiritual growth. When we prioritize these principles in the cycle of spiritual growth, we deepen, establish and refine our spiritual identity.

Prayer Focus:
Review the Vision statement and your personal ratings, then use your own evaluation as a tool for prayer. Use each of the "I am" statements as a platform to request the Lord's help to become more of each, or to celebrate what you are. For example:

"Lord, I am not as loving as I would like to be. I can see that I have not made this a priority in my life, please help me to grow in my ability to love."

Use the space below to write out your prayer.

Vision & Strategy

The church described in the New Testament knows nothing of a Christian who is not a disciple committed to a local body of believers. The teaching of Christ and His followers makes it very clear that the local church is God's instrument for getting the Gospel into our hearts and lives and into the world. When this happens, it creates an ongoing cycle of spiritual life and growth.

You were made to Connect, Grow, and Serve as a member of the body of Christ. When you engage in this cycle of obedience, you experience a natural process for growth.

There are two primary reasons why this can fail to happen: 1) We get distracted from who we are (as God's children); and 2) We don't know what we are supposed to be doing. By the end of this Devotional, you will have an action plan for spiritual growth.

Without knowing who God has created us to be, we inadvertently conform to the culture around us. This is at the heart of the Christian journey – discovering and establishing our true spiritual identity.

Four facts about this spiritual growth and the cycle of spiritual growth:
1. Spiritual development is not automatic
2. Spiritual development is a process
3. Spiritual development isn't the same as spiritual giftedness
4. Spiritual development takes discipline

Over the next few days, we will look at each of these to help us better understand this spiritual journey which began when we accepted a relationship with Christ.

Spiritual development is not automatic.

The Bible describes spiritual growth in the same manner that we describe physiological growth. Look closely at the following passages and paragraph, then write a sentence that describes your understanding about spiritual growth not being automatic.

Hebrews 5:12-13 says: *"You have been Christians for a long time now, and you ought to be teaching others, but instead…you need someone to teach you…When a person is still living on milk, it shows he isn't very far along in his Christian life…He's still a baby Christian!"*

Notice what He says should take place by this time in these believers' lives. One goal of spiritual development is that every believer is spiritually reproductive. When we cannot teach or give away what we've received, our growth has been arrested.

Ephesians 4:14-15 *"Then we will no longer be infants, tossed back and forth by the waves, and blown here and there by every wind of teaching and by the cunning and craftiness of men in their deceitful scheming. Instead speaking the truth in love we will in all things grow up into Him who is the head, that is Christ. From Him the whole body, joined and held together by every supporting ligament, grows and builds itself up in love, as each part does its work."*

How does the Ephesians passage describe the condition of spiritual immaturity?

I jokingly say that you are only young once, but you can be immature forever! Many are physically mature, but emotionally immature. Peter Scazzero describes in his book, *Emotionally Healthy Spirituality*: "You cannot be spiritually mature and be emotionally immature." We have unfortunately neglected the kind of spiritual development that produces emotionally mature people. Somewhere along the way we became confused, thinking that if people knew more, they would be more Christ-like. Spiritual information does not automatically produce spiritual transformation. The result of spiritual immaturity is instability and irresponsibility in relationships.

Oswald Chambers says: "God can give you a pure heart in an instant but he cannot quickly bring you Christian character (maturity). That takes time and can come only through a series of right choices."

In your own words write a sentence that describes why this is so important to remember and why our culture struggles against this truth.

Prayer Focus:
Ask the Lord to empower you with the Spirit of self-control.
2 Timothy 1:7 says *"God has not given us a Spirit of timidity, but of power, of love and of self-control."* To move into *consistent* spiritual growth (because it is not automatic) we need His Spirit to have more control over us than our human flesh. Speak to Him and ask:

"Lord Jesus fill me with your Spirit; give me a supernatural desire to act on truth and to grow more in love with you and your purposes for my life."

Vision & Strategy

Spiritual development is a process.

From my childhood, I can remember wanting to grow up more quickly. As the youngest of four boys, I was constantly watching my older brothers do things without including me! To which my mother would say: "You are not old enough. When you grow up you can do those things. Your honeymoon is coming." I didn't know what a honeymoon was, but it had to be good because being left behind surely wasn't! Growing up spiritually is also a process. It takes time and we need certain experiences to grow up in a healthy way.

Read the following passages and paragraph, circling the words that stand out to you about "process", and then write a sentence that describes what you see about the process of growth.

Proverbs 8:5 (GN) says: *"Learn to be mature."*

2 Peter 3:18 says: *"Continue to grow in the grace and knowledge of our Savior Jesus Christ."*

If children fail to learn how to respect and obey parental authority, they will struggle to function well in every other context where such respect is critical. Something in their developmental process was interrupted or underdeveloped. When this happens, they cannot go back and be a child in their parents' home again and pick up where they left off (although many young adults do return home because of these deficits) but they can re-engage the process of learning in order to cultivate an ability to be respectful. Just as a child crawls before walking, and walks before running, so we grow in steps over time. If we had a child whose development was stunted, we would search for resources and tools to help them get back on the path of healthy growth. When we resist the process of growth, spiritually and emotionally, we encounter relational setbacks. When individuals never step into the process, they experience a series of relationships that fail to thrive. Regrettably, this can go on indefinitely. Spiritual development is a process.

In your own words write a sentence about why spiritual development is a process.

Spiritual development isn't the same as spiritual giftedness.

This is a challenging truth to embrace because we all love to see and observe gifted people. Our culture makes this mistake consistently. If salespeople bring in the big dollars, then management will overlook their transgressions because they are "producers". If an actor commands the stage, no one even seems to care that they are going through marriages like shoes. If a singer can hit the high notes, their alcohol abuse is tolerated or even ignored. The operating principle of the world is, "If their aberrant behavior doesn't affect their performance, it doesn't matter. The show must go on."

The Corinthian church in the New Testament was the prime example of this issue. 1 Corinthians 1:7 tells us that they did *"...not lack any spiritual gift..."*, and yet they were the most dysfunctional and immature church. 1 Corinthians. 3:1 Paul says: *"I could not address you as spiritual but as worldly – mere infants in Christ."*

There is nothing wrong with youth (1 Tm. 4:12-13), but there is something very wrong when we ignore childish behavior just because someone is gifted. Childish reactions create power struggles, poor listeners, temper tantrums and passive aggressive/pouty behavior. Paul instructs them in chapter 1: *"When I was a child I talked like a child, I thought like a child, I reasoned like a child. When I became a man I put childish ways behind me."*

In your own words, why is it important to see the difference between spiritual development and spiritual gifting?

Prayer Focus:
Take a moment and thank God for the growth you've experienced, and ask Him to show you how you can be engaged in the process of becoming more Christ-like and more emotionally mature.

Spiritual Disciplines

Today, we look at a fourth fact of spiritual development. We will take three days to look at a fundamental and critical ingredient in our strategy – spiritual disciplines. So find a good place to settle in. Don't rush. Everything we employ in our strategy for spiritual growth will be built upon these days. This foundation will empower you to step into the cycle of spiritual life and growth you desire.

Spiritual development takes discipline.

Wouldn't it be nice to delete this point? I mean really, we have to be disciplined to grow up? Spiritually and emotionally, yes. This is one of the reasons why we have well-meaning families that have children who struggle to become mature. In some cases, parenting style might have lacked the healthy blend of love and discipline required to teach children to be responsible in their duties, behavior and attitudes. If we lacked this kind of discipline – not the kind where your father constantly spanked you, but the kind where he patiently trained you – then we might be very dutiful, yet lack a joyful presence. It's the difference between being responsible because I have to, and being responsible because I want to. They can look the same at a glance, but are entirely different upon examination.

1 Timothy 4:7-8
"Have nothing to do with godless myths and old wives' tales; rather, train yourself to be godly. For physical training is of some value, but godliness has value for all things, holding promise for both the present life and the life to come."

Hebrews 12:11
"At the time, discipline isn't much fun. It always feels like it's going against the grain. Later, of course, it pays off handsomely, for it's the well-trained who find themselves mature in their relationship with God." (MSG)

Proverbs 12:1
"If you love learning, you love the discipline that goes with it – how shortsighted to refuse correction!" (MSG)

The New Testament term for "Christ followers" might surprise you. It is not the word "Christian." There is nothing wrong with being called a Christian; it's just not how the early believers were known. Most of us remember that Jesus called people to be his followers; that is, "disciples." The word "Christian" is found only 3 times in the New Testament; whereas the word "disciple" is used 269 times. It refers to one who is a "pupil" or "learner." The New Testament was written by disciples, about disciples, for disciples.

The concepts of discipleship and being disciplined are inextricably linked. They share the same root word. History tells us that the Early Church (Christ followers) practiced spiritual disciplines to help them conform to Christ's teaching, character and mission.

A discipline is a means to an end. The end is to be Christ-like (spiritually mature); yielding to His will and surrendering our control. Spiritual disciplines teach us to bring our bodies, minds, attitudes and relationships under the control of the Holy Spirit.

Let's look at our spiritual disciplines and see how they fit into our strategy. Here is my definition for a spiritual discipline:

"A discipline is something that I can do now that will enable me, in the future, to be able to accomplish what I otherwise could not do."

Here are a couple more definitions:

"A deliberately self-imposed habit that nurtures spiritual health and fosters spiritual growth leading to maturity." Douglas Rumford

"The Spiritual Disciplines are those personal and corporate disciplines that promote spiritual growth. They are the habits of devotion and experiential Christianity that have been practiced by the people of God since biblical times." Douglas Whitney

The interesting thing about disciplines is that they are the keys to proficiency at anything of value. A musician cannot just step up to an instrument and make beautiful music. It requires practice and dedication. Athletes function at a winning level when they dedicate time to refine their abilities. Why would we think it would be any different as a Christ follower?

The concept of following Jesus wasn't just that He was cool to be around. I am sure He was, but it was much more than that. His followers watched every move, every interaction, the way He handled pressure, verbal attack or criticism. They took in how He played, laughed and conversed with those around Him; the way He behaved around authority figures, common people, sick people and children.
I believe this is exactly what He invited his followers to do in Matthew 11:28-30 (MSG):

"Are you tired, worn out, burned out on religion? Come to me, get away with me and you will recover your life. Walk with me, work with me, watch how I do it. Learn the unforced rhythms of grace."

Have you noticed how skilled athletes, musicians or communicators make their craft look easy? We learn to die to our flesh and live under His control; living out His presence in a way that shows grace and kindness. Being competent at anything significant requires discipline and focus. That's what happens when we learn to follow Jesus well.

Before you wrap up today's devotional, write down my definition of a "discipline". Can you remember it? If not, review it and then write it out in the space given.

A Discipline:

Next, write down two or three things that you have learned to do well (that you have been disciplined in learning). If you are struggling to think of something you do well, ask a close friend or family member for their opinions. An example of some things might be knowledge of some topic, like sports or a given hobby. Another could be an area of personal competency used at your place of employment.

1.

2.

3.

Prayer Focus:
Express gratitude for the things that you have learned to do well. Ask the Lord to help you to want to be as disciplined and focused in your walk with Him, as you have done with these other areas of competency.

Week In Review Questions

1. On day 11, we considered our Mission as a church — why we exist. How do you see our Mission being illustrated in the life of Jesus? How are you learning to meet people where they are and to love them to where Christ wants them to be?

2. On day 12, we completed a self-assessment for personally living out our YC Vision. Share how you rated yourself on each of the five "I am" statements and why?

3. On day 13, Pastor Jeff gave the first (of four) facts about Spiritual development. *1) It is not automatic.*
How have you seen this fact displayed in your own life? Why is this a counter cultural fact?

4. On Day 14, we looked at the second and third facts; *2) Spiritual development is a process* and *3) It isn't the same as spiritual giftedness.* What stood out to you about these two facts?

5. The fourth fact was that Spiritual development requires discipline. What do you think about this concept and how significant do you think the "spiritual disciplines" are for us as believers? Can you say (remember) Pastor Jeff's definition of a discipline? Why would remembering the definition of a discipline be important?

Week 4

This week we will dig deep into one of the most critical habits needed to effectively walk in the Spirit. I call this the "Critical link". Learning to be "self-aware" is at the heart of being able to *die to self* (Mk 8:35) or *"put to death, whatever belongs to the earthly nature"* (Cl 3:5). This will require you to learn a new set of skills that can empower you to better distinguish between what is from God – that you will learn to feed and cultivate, and what comes from the flesh and this world – that you will learn to put off and eliminate.

Spiritual Disciplines

Spiritual Disciplines assist me in developing Christ-like virtue & character.

When teaching on spiritual disciplines, I often write on a whiteboard three major Biblical categories as important aspects of the life of a believer (disciple or Christian).

Christian Doctrine......Christian practices......Christian virtue......

Unfortunately, we often use these terms interchangeably. So let's clear up the confusion. Christian *doctrine* is what we believe (the Trinity – Father, Son & Spirit), the atoning work of Christ's death, the infilling presence of the Spirit etc...and for each doctrine we have a chapter and verse. Christian *virtue*, on the other hand, is about our behavior (kindness, patience, integrity, Christian character). Here's the deal, I cannot get to Christian virtue and character by knowing all there is to know about Christian doctrine. Knowing doctrine doesn't make me any more Christ-like than knowing all about basketball makes me an NBA star! In fact, Satan might know more doctrine than you. If I want to live a virtuous Christ-like life, I have to employ Christian (spiritual) *practices, disciplines, and habits* to get there.

Spiritual Disciplines are habits or practices that sharpen my focus on Christ and affect change in my heart.

Charlie Nobel said it well: "First we make our habits, and then our habits make us."

Spiritual Disciplines are means to an end.

When we practice the disciplines they equip us to do what the New Testament authors called "walking in" or "keeping in step with the Spirit."

Galatians 5:24: *"Those who belong to Christ Jesus have crucified the sinful nature with it' passions and desires. Since we live by the Spirit, let us keep in step with the Spirit. Let us not become conceited, provoking and angering each other."*

We have all had experiences where we have tried but just couldn't master something. This is where many believers live. They feel frustrated because they feel like they can't pray well, witness well, articulate their faith well. So, they resign themselves to rely on professional Christian leaders, pastors and authors to articulate their faith for them. They can recommend a helpful Christian book or podcast, but they are ineffective to live out a courageous spiritual life themselves. My friends, this should not be the case!

Spiritual Disciplines empower us to accomplish the Great Commission.

Dallas Willard, who has influenced me as much as anyone on this, describes this conundrum as the -Great Omission-:

"In the place of Christ's plan, (Mt 28:19-20) a historical drift has substituted: Make converts (to a particular faith and practice) and baptize them into church membership. This shift has caused two great omissions from the Great Commission to stand out. Most important we start by omitting the making of disciples or enrolling people as Christ's students….We also omit taking our converts through training that will bring them ever increasingly to do what Jesus directed."

Spiritual Disciplines equip us for life's challenges.

Spiritual disciplines – our pathway for turning our want – to into our will-do. Spiritual disciplines are the habits I bring to the mundane moments of life, so I can better sustain an awareness of God's presence in the painful moments of life. For example, when I create space to practice solitude, prayer, gratitude, meditation, memorization and study in the mundane moments of life, I equip myself to sense and respond to His presence during times of deep challenge and pain.

Spiritual Disciplines are motivated by love, not for love.

It is important to point out a potential danger or misunderstanding about spiritual disciplines. Our flesh (ego) can hijack anything, including spiritual disciplines. If we become rigid or judgmental as we employ a set of disciplines, then something is askew. We do not practice the disciplines so God will like us more. He already loves us. We do them so we can be more like Him. We do not do the them so we can get God's attention; we do them to train ourselves to pay better attention to His presence in our lives. We are not trying to earn God's love. His love for us is never the issue; it is our love for Him that regularly falters and needs refinement.

Tomorrow, we will look at a critical link to tie the disciplines into our strategy – the "cycle of spiritual life and growth". As we wrap up today, write what you have learned about spiritual disciplines. What stood out to you as important to remember?

Your thoughts:

Prayer Focus:
Continue to express gratitude for something you are learning. Thank God for His unconditional love and imagine what it would be like to be ever mindful of His love until it becomes your primary motivation in life. What might that look like?

The Critical Link

Growing in self-awareness so I can deny myself and take up my cross.

Mark 8:34-35: *"Then Jesus called the crowd to him, along with his disciples and said, "If anyone would come after me he must deny himself and take up his cross and follow me. For whoever wants to save his life will lose it, but whoever loses his life for me and for the Gospel will*
save it."

Dallas Willard in his classic work, *The Spirit of the Disciplines,* says: "The disciplines are what bring our body's under His power." They assist us in the work of denying self and living unto Christ. How can I put Jesus in first place if I am already there? We cannot accomplish the work of Christ if our own agenda keeps getting in the way. Douglas Rumford, a pastor and passionate practitioner of spiritual disciplines, says: "...spiritual self-awareness marks our journey toward Christlikeness...which drives us further up and further in to God."

I have been living with myself for a long time. And what I have discovered is that I can very easily be my own worst enemy. There is no way that I can get out of the way if I don't realize that I am in the way.

At the very heart of following Jesus is His call to stop following ourselves. This is about as counterintuitive as you can get. We have been going to Burger King from the time we could sit up in a booster chair, hearing "Have it your way", and boy, is that how we live! Our effort to get what we want can often be at odds with what the Spirit wants.

Galatians 5:17: *"The sinful nature desires what is contrary to the Spirit and the Spirit is contrary to the sinful nature. They are in conflict with each other, so that you do not do what you want."*

Research confirms what Scripture has been saying. A University of Chicago research team found that "those who demonstrate more self-control were more satisfied than those who gave into their wants more often. It may seem counterintuitive, but those who answered yes to statements like, 'I do certain things that are bad for me, if they are fun,' felt dismayed more often than those who lived a life of greater self-denial," according to an article in the *Journal of Personality* study.

This has been understood for centuries, Plato said: "The first and greatest victory is to conquer self." Napoleon Hill remarked: "If you cannot conquer self, you will be conquered by self." In his excellent book, *As A Man Thinketh*, written at the turn of the last century, James Allen challenges the reader: "The selfishness must be discovered and understood before it can be removed. It is powerless to remove itself. Neither will it disappear of itself. Darkness ceases only when light is introduced; so ignorance can only be dispersed by knowledge; selfishness by love."

Growing in healthy self-awareness is impossible to do without employing the disciplines of self-examination (which helps us to discover our selfishness), meditation, and solitude. Until we realize that God did not design us to go nonstop, we will continue to fill our lives with activity that inadvertently takes us away from the awareness needed to yield and surrender ourselves to Him.

Several years ago I heard about the Pleasure/Pain Principle that motivates us. Each of us, at an unconscious level, is motivated by one of two things – either to avoid pain or to experience gain (or pleasure). To become self-aware is to have the objectivity to recognize what motivates you toward any given decision. Here's how the Pain/Pleasure principle might look in the life of an average Joe.

Joe sleeps in because he doesn't want to leave his warm bed – pleasure. He jumps out of bed and frantically runs out the door for work because he doesn't want to be fired – pain. He grabs an apple fritter at a donut shop along the way because he's hungry – pleasure. He feels guilty because he's overweight and out of shape – pain. He argues with a coworker because he wants to be right–pleasure. He feel bad because his coworker won't speak to him – pain. He's late for lunch with his spouse because his boss was talking to him and he wants his approval – pleasure. He feels bad that his spouse is upset with him for being late – pain. He stops by the bar on the way home to have some drinks with some friends – pleasure. He feels sad that his spouse is again upset with him for being late and now drunk – pain.

What Joe doesn't see is that both pain and pleasure are at work in his motivation. Without a deeper awareness, he will struggle to know when he needs to face pain (instead of avoid it) and when he needs to say "no" instead of "yes" to pleasure.

Our sin nature operates at this level, and even after conversion, it is often stronger than our spirit. God wants us to discover a new set of motivations that are not held captive by our aversion to pain or obsession with pleasure.

Becoming self-aware happens when we recognize our motives and what drives them. Until we are skilled in this area we will often feel caught in the middle of a spiritual struggle that leaves us feeling more defeated than victorious. Gaining the insight to discern what drives us (either our flesh or the Spirit), will take time, solitude, examination, meditation on truth, and learning to walk in the Spirit.

The good news is that God has given us His Spirit of Truth (Jn 16:13), and has promised to live within us (Jn 14:18). This Spirit can lead us into truth, comfort us, convict, guide and lead us into a new set of beliefs and behaviors that will actually produce an amazing collection of qualities: love, joy, peace, patience, kindness, goodness, faithfulness, gentleness, and self-control (Jn 16; Ga 5).

Charles Swindoll says: "An inner restlessness grows within us when we refuse to get alone and examine our own hearts, including our motives…Unless we get alone for the hard work of self-examination in times of solitude, serenity will remain only a distant dream."

As we grow spiritually, we need to realize that it is normal to experience pleasure or pain. One is not good and the other bad. In fact, God wants to use pain to help us grow (Rm 5:3-5) and He gives us all kinds of pleasure that can be a blessing (1 Tm 4:4). Walking in the Spirit is being tuned-in to who He calls us to become and what He calls us to do, not being driven by a motivation to avoid pain or indulge in pleasure. If I cannot overcome (put to death) my compulsion to avoid pain and experience pleasure, I will find it extremely difficult to take up my cross and follow Jesus.

Take a few minutes and write out some of the things that you feel compelled to do that are motivated by either experiencing pleasure or avoiding pain. Consider your relationship with sex, food, drink, entertainment, work, play, friends, exercise and spiritual activity.

PLEASURE   PAIN

Being self-aware empowers us to recognize when "self" is getting in the way of healthy Spirit-led decisions. Look closely at the following quotes and write under each one how it applies to the Pain/Pleasure principle and/or learning to die to your sinful/natural desires.

Unknown author: "Solitude is a terrible trial, for it serves to crack open and burst apart the shell of our superficial securities."
Your observation:

Bishop Wilson: "Those who deny themselves will be sure to find their strength increased, their affections raised, and their inward peace continually augmented."
Your observation:

Thomas a Kempis: "He who knows best how to suffer will keep the greater peace, that man is conqueror of himself, friend of Christ, heir of heaven."
Your observation:

Write a sentence or two about what you think these quotes have in common with the Mark 8:34-35 passage that we studied earlier.

What do you think the notion of self-awareness has to do with spiritual disciplines and becoming more like Christ?

Prayer Focus:
Close out your time today by praying through this well-known passage that affirms the need for greater self-awareness.

Psalm 139:23-24 *"Search me, O God and know my heart; test me and know my anxious thoughts. See if there is any offensive way in me, and lead me in the way everlasting."*

The Critical Link

Today we continue to look closely at how spiritual disciplines can help us to cultivate greater self-awareness. As we do so, look at the following passages and make a few observations about each of them:

According to the following passages where is our struggle, what feeds the struggle and what is the goal (desired outcome) as we overcome the struggle?

Ephesians 4:22-24

Galatians 5:16-24

Romans 12:2

When Jesus said: *"the truth will set you free."* (Jn 8:31-32), He was not saying hearing truth or being exposed to truth will create freedom. Rather, the goal is to know the truth so deeply that it retrains the way we think, believe and behave. This is what the apostle Paul affirms when he tells us that we need to undergo training (1 Tm 4:7-8).

Scott Peck says it as well as I have ever heard it:

> "What does a life of total dedication to the truth mean? It means, first of all, a life of continuous and never ending self-examination.
>
> To have such discipline we must be totally dedicated to the truth. That is to say we must always hold the truth, as best as we can determine it, to be more important, more vital to our self-interest than our comfort. Conversely, we must always consider our personal discomfort relatively unimportant and, indeed even welcome it in the service and search for truth.
>
> When one is dedicated to the truth this pain seems relatively unimportant – and less and less important (and therefore less and less painful) the further we proceed on the path of self-examination."

When we combine the habits of solitude, self-examination, confession, and meditation of God's truth, they empower us to have and experience an ongoing transformation of our hearts and minds. We move away from our natural compulsion to avoid pain and seek pleasure, and into a new paradigm where we face pain and find pleasure from obedience and walking in the truth/Spirit. In this new place of God's presence and acceptance, we learn to become more comfortable with discomfort. Each of the passages above reminds us that we have a propensity, within our sinful nature and the patterns of the world, to be deceived and trapped by beliefs that prevent us from living the life we have been invited to live.

Few of us are comfortable with healthy self-examination. This might be due to the fact that we are already habituated toward unhealthy internal-examination. The critical link of self-awareness is not an easy concept to understand or employ. Not because it isn't true or a worthy skill, but because we have never been taught how to do it. The irony is that our negative and critical thoughts about ourselves or others happen ever so naturally, with no conscious effort! Healthy self-examination means searching our private thoughts and beliefs with the Spirit of truth at our side (or better yet, in our hearts), leading us into new levels of freedom.

Here are some examples of thought patterns that might need to be "put off" or "transformed". Write under each one what you think the corrective thought, based on God's word/truth, might be. I've done the first as an example.

— <u>Resistance to change</u> — "I don't want to change because the change doesn't feel like "me." Or, "it doesn't feel comfortable".

Corrective thought: When Jesus calls me to repent — turn and change — It brings me into a new set of thoughts and behaviours that at first may not "feel natural" because they are new. Through obedience and perseverance the change can lead me to a new normal.

— <u>Holding on to hurt</u> — "I can't believe they would do (or say) that to me. I can't believe they could be so insensitive and clueless!"

Corrective thought:

— <u>A prideful spirit</u> — "I am so much better than the little credit I've been given — They are missing the boat!" Or, "I am not going to admit that I feel insecure and like a fake. I'm not going to risk rejection."

Corrective thought:

— <u>Avoidance of pain</u> — "I am uncomfortable (this is usually a foggy notion), where can I go to (drink, use the drug of my choice, view pornography, or manipulate someone) so I can feel better right now?"

Corrective thought:

– <u>Medicating our wounds</u> – " If no one knows what I am doing (any unhealthy form of medication) it's not really a problem."

Corrective thought:

– <u>Other people make me angry</u> – "Other people push my buttons and then I am really angry."

Corrective thought:

Are there any distorted thoughts, beliefs or negative patterns that you struggle with that need to be "put off" not mentioned above? What are they and what might your corrective belief/truth be?

Prayer Focus:
Ask the Lord to continue to give you deeper insight into your own thought patterns and deceitful desires. Ask Him to equip you to do the self-examination Scripture calls us to do. The Lord wants you to experience greater and greater levels of freedom and victory that can only come from renewal of your mind.

The Critical Link

Have you ever caught yourself progressively obsessing over something someone said or did to you? Or have you ever found yourself locked onto a personal opinion that takes on a life of its own? You can't seem to stop thinking about it and the weight of your own opinion and perception becomes a source of anxiety. Many times the very thing upon which we are ruminating isn't even founded in reality, but rather just our mistaken perception. For some reason, we deceive ourselves into thinking we are expert mind readers and can interpret the motives and intentions of others. This is a nuance to our flesh (our sinful nature), which is why we find it so "natural." The KJV Bible describes this as coming from the "natural man" (1 Co 2:4). Jesus wants every believer to learn to do something that is unnatural to our flesh. He wants us to search our heart, mind, thoughts and beliefs through the light of His truth. We all have a healthy desire to be known, loved and valued; but our flesh and deceitful desires twist our motives.

Jesus calls us to die to the sinful nature ("natural man" or "flesh") (Mk 8:34-35); but if we cannot discern between what originates from our flesh or the Spirit, we won't know what we should be trying to "starve" and what we should be trying to "feed." When we feed the wrong one, the result is more anxiety, dissension, gossip, and spiritual and emotional strife. If you think this isn't an issue, you are struggling with self-awareness. This is an issue for everyone. The real question is: "Can I see how this issue is affecting my life/thoughts and relationships, and what am I doing about it?"

To put this to work, let's look at an acronym that I have modified slightly, (originally developed by cognitive psychologist Albert Ellis in the 1940s) and can help us apply the Biblical truth of transforming the mind through God's revelation. I will refer to this approach as the "ABC model of change." Which can enable us to identify and transform our thoughts to match God's truth, which can set us free."

A + B = C

A – stands for **Activating event**. This could be any number of things that might be mildly or severely perceived as negative – receiving personal criticism, failing to complete a project, being stood up for a meeting, being ignored by someone you esteem, being the victim of a crime, or being lied to by a friend or spouse.

B –stands for **Belief system** – what you tell yourself about that event. This is where the work comes in; learning to recognize your self-talk (through self-examination). If you are telling yourself something that isn't aligned with God's revealed truth, you will become ensnared by a lie – deception will set in and Satan will rob you of God's joy, peace and the discernment about how to behave or respond to the event.

C – stands for **Consequent emotion**. Here is a helpful tip. We tend to recognize our negative emotions before we can discern our wrong thinking or "belief." The middle piece (the B-Belief) of this equation is the most illusive. When you are growing in the skill of "self-examination," you will be more equipped to take every thought captive and bring it under the Lordship of Christ (2 Co 5:4) and respond out of obedience to Christ instead of our woundedness and flesh. This isn't psycho mumbo – jumbo. This is spiritual warfare. The Bible makes it clear that the battle is in your mind; and if you don't train it, the enemy will pummel your thoughts with lies.

Today and tomorrow, we will look closely at how this method can assist us to conquer our flesh and recognize how the patterns of this world have been distorting how we think, what we tell ourselves and what we believe.

Self-examination becomes your critical link when you learn to arrest any given circumstance (activating event), and reaction (consequent emotion or behavior fueled by that emotion) that is disrupting your ability to respond in a Christ like manner.

Here's an example: Steve has just been confronted by a new co-worker who tells Steve that he comes across as overbearing, struggles to listens and seems to always want to have his way. Steve feels angry and defensive and tells his team mate that "he doesn't know him, he's not been here long enough to give that kind of feedback and he should keep his thoughts to himself." Later that evening Steve finds himself ruminating on the unpleasant interaction and comes to the conclusion that the new employee has been talking to Sally, another co-worker that he knows doesn't like him, because of the way she always clams up, everytime he's around.

Even though Steve is a believer most of those around him do not sense a heart of love but rather a very self absorbed person who thinks he's always right.

Let's see if we can use our ABC tool to assess some of what might be going on under the surface for Steve.

Taking our thoughts captive, and learning to respond from the Spirit, and not our flesh, is an unnatural skill. Which means we have to do something new. We recognize that we need to do something different when we experience something painful or uncomfortable, especially in our relationships. When we feel upset, sad, angry or anxious it should be like a light on our spiritual dashboard. Just as an oil light tells you something may be wrong with your engine, your negative emotions are telling you that something may be wrong with your perceptions, beliefs, or self-talk concerning some circumstance or event.

Looking back at Steve's story we can see several things. Let's start with the "Consequent emotion". We start here because most of us are not very aware of what we believe or what we tell ourselves from event to event, but we are aware when we are feeling negative emotions (frustration, anger, anxiety etc).

What are Steve's emotions? Anger and defensive, right? That's his "C" (Consequent emotion)

What was the Activating event? His team mate confronting him with some concerns about the way he comes across.

Now, which of the following "Misbeliefs (lies) might be fueling what Steve is telling himself (self-talk) which led to his negative emotions and reactive behavior?

- If I fail, I am a failure.
- Any criticism is a sign of failure.
- I need to be the most knowledgeable in my job.
- I can tell what others are thinking.

Which misbeliefs did you select as potentially fueling Steve's negative emotions and reactive behavior? If you picked all of them, you are correct. Most of them are a form of what one author calls the "Performance trap." I need to perform at some illusive level (somewhere close to perfect as evidenced by praise and the lack of criticism) to feel good about myself. The last one is a classic misbelief that says we can accurately mind-read what others are thinking.

It is much more comfortable to analyze Steve rather than ourselves; but just maybe, by taking Steve through our ABC method, you might gain a little insight into yourself. Is there a personal point of connection Steve's story? Have you ever felt like you have to perform to be accepted, loved or valued? Write your answers below.

If you were going to correct Steve's misbeliefs from God's word/truth, where would you start? What Scriptures or biblical truths might help you to counsel Steve to think differently about his "Activating event" (what he tells himself about others giving him input that he may not like)?

Prayer Focus:
Ask the Lord to reveal to you any heavy or negative emotions that might help you begin to see where some misbeliefs and lies (from the enemy) have been stealing your joy.

The Critical Link

Let's continue to put our new tool into practice. We will add a little more to our new acronym – ABC & **DE** model for change: **Destructive choices or behavior** are likely to follow. Therefore, we need to **Examine & Exchange** what we are telling ourselves; learning to replace the misbelief with God's truth.

When King David prayed: *"Search me, oh God, and know my heart; test me and know my anxious thoughts."* He was engaged in what we call the discipline of self-examination. When Jeremiah (the prophet) called us to *"Examine and test our ways…"* (La 3:40), it was because we have a propensity to choose the path that our flesh would rather take. When Jeremiah declared that *"the heart is deceitful and beyond cure, who can understand it"* (Je 17:9), he was urging us to take personal ownership of our vulnerability of being deceived by untruth that feeds our human nature (flesh). The New Testament authors affirm the same concept. Paul told the Ephesians: *"You were taught with regard to your former way of life to put off the old self, which is being corrupted by its deceitful desires…"* and to the Corinthians, *"take every thought captive to make it obedient to Christ."*

We will never be victorious in a battle we're unwilling to face. In the above passages, notice how both Paul and Jeremiah point out our "deceitful" side. When we increase our awareness of how susceptible we are to being deceived by a misbelief (Belief system) we actually become better equipped to identify that misbelief and defeat it more quickly.

We are all vulnerable to a host of misbeliefs, but we usually have one or two that wreak greater havoc in our lives. Let's zero-in on some of the most common misbeliefs and see if we can identify one or two in your "bag of tricks." It is a mark of maturity to see when we want good things for wrong reasons. Have any of these masked motives or misbeliefs ever lurked in the shadows of your heart? Read through this short list and circle any that ring true for you:

Spiritual Misbeliefs Driven By Our Flesh & The Patterns Of This World

— *Fear of failure* — I am a failure I fail (or receive criticism).

— *Shame* — I am what I am. I cannot change, I am hopeless.

— *Blame* — I am unworthy of love and deserve to be punished.

— *Adrenaline Addict* — I need excitement or something risky to feel energized and alive.

— *Fear of conflict* — Conflict is bad and needs to be avoided.

— *Fear of emotions* — Negative emotions are bad and need to be avoided.

— *Performance trap* — I must perform at a high level in order to be accepted or feel good about myself.

— *Compartmentalizing* — It doesn't matter what I do if no one knows or gets hurt.

— *Can't slow down* — I must be doing something (or being productive) in order to feel good about myself.

— *Approval addict* — I must have the approval (or attention) of certain others in order to feel good about myself.

— *Denial* — The past is the past, just forget it; or I don't have any (serious) problems.

— *Judgemental spirit* — others make mistakes and deserve to be punished.

— *Materialism* — I must have material things in order to be valuable and happy.

Now that you have selected a few personal misbeliefs, take a few minutes with each one and write down some possible "Activating events" that could trigger your misbelief and the "consequent emotions." Paying attention to the emotional response could serve as a light on your spiritual dashboard, helping you to recognize that you are operating in the flesh. When any of the above misbeliefs influence your emotions, they can pull you away from God's truth and draw you into "destructive unhealthy behavior." Everything from pouting, outbursts of anger, divisive conversations, gossip, factions, pornography, sexual misconduct, envy or selfish ambition (Ga 5:19-21). In the space below, place your misbelief next to the "B" and then list several potential events (things that trigger unhealthy choices and behavior) next to the "A". Then try to identify some of the emotions that rise up in you next to the "C," followed by the kind of destructive behavior might follow. I filled in the first one with one of my own misbeliefs that I am learning to defeat (performance trap).

After we have identified the ABC&D of this exercise we will go back and finish the process by adding the "E" – "Examine and Exchange" the misbelief for what God says is true. Take your time through this process, it will equip you to learn how to identify your misbeliefs and correct your thoughts through God's truth (2 Co 5:3-5).

A My misbelief could be triggered by criticism, a negative comment, or someone expressing disappointment in me.
B Performance trap – I must perform at a high level to be accepted or feel good about myself.
C My emotional response will usually be anger, anxiety, sadness, or feeling depressed.
D Destructive or unhealthy behavior could follow. I could become defensive, isolate, do negative mind reading, and/or be tempted to medicate my wounded ego.

A

B

C

D

A

B

C

D

Once you have identified the untruth/misbelief, you are now able to *"take every thought captive and make it obedient to Christ."* (2 Co 5:4), correcting the misbelief with the truth revealed in Scripture. Ask the Holy Spirit to help you to know what God says about your 'Belief system" and seek His counsel/word to renew your mind. The following list of truth statements are to assist you as you replace your misbelief with God's truth. Circle the ones that address your most prominent misbeliefs and place them in the "E" position. The corresponding Scripture would be a valuable text upon which to meditate and commit to memory. This is how we can identify and transform our mind in the very moments of our struggles.

Spiritual Truth Statements For Renewing & Transforming Our Mind

– God loves me unconditionally regardless of my performance (Ro 5:6-8, 8:35-39).

– Jesus has taken my punishment, therefore I do not need to punish myself or fear rejection (Ro 8:1; 1 Jn 4:18).

– Because of God's love and acceptance I don't need other's approval to feel positive about myself (1 Sa 7:16; Ga 2:6).

– I can become humble, gentle and loving to others through His Spirit in me (Ep 4:2; Ga 5:22-23).

– I can take responsibility for mistakes in a way that honors God and builds trust with others (Ja 5:16; Ga 6:1-4; Ep 4:29-32).

– My sins have been forgiven but my behavior can have consequences. Therefore I can learn to change and honor God in my choices (Ga 5:13-17, 6:7-9).

– I can take healthy pride in my personal growth without comparing myself to others (Ga 6:3-4).

– I can forgive others from my judgement and offer God's acceptance (Ro 12;14-21, 15:7; Co 3:12-14).

– I am loved and God's Spirit is helping me to grow and change (Jn 14:16-21; Ep 2:8-10).

– It is healthy and essential to slow down to soak up His presence and truth (Ps 46:10)

Now Examine and Exchange your misbelief with the "Truth" statement that you selected. Here is my example:
E God loves me unconditionally regardless of my perfomance (Ro 5:6-8, 8:35-39)

E

E

One of the most difficult battles you will fight in spiritual warfare is the battle against pride.

Pride will sabotage your ability to own areas of personal vulnerability. *Humility*, in contrast, will empower you to take ownership of your susceptibility to be tricked (deceived) into a stubborn resistance to do the work of self-examination. Napoleon Hill reminds us that: "If you cannot conquer self, you will be conquered by self."

Our misbeliefs (and the battle we fight to overcome them) come from two primary fronts – our own sinful (deceptive) nature (Ga 5:13-26, 6:7-9) and the world we live in, ruled by the evil one (Ro 12:2; Ep 6:10-18). Both of these battles are fought through the power of God's truth and His Spirit's presence in us. The way Satan works is through deception; he is the father of lies (Jn 8:44). Therefore, our method (the ABCDE model for change) is a powerful way to put on the "helmet of salvation" and take up the "sword of the Spirit" – the word of God. When we learn to defeat pride and walk in humility, we can advance our ability to experience spiritual victory on a daily basis.

Our journey toward great emotional/spiritual health and freedom will require a commitment to practice these new habits and disciplines in order to experience the freedom that Jesus offers us. When you adopt and refine a daily connection with God through prayer and Bible engagement, a regular time to grow with others in healthy spiritual community, and then serve as an overflow of Christ's life in you, this freedom will become a more powerful reality.

Remember that our thoughts reflect what we believe, even if it is a lie, myth, or misbelief.

Prayer Focus:
Ask Jesus to reveal to you some of your predominate misbeliefs and how His truth, love, forgiveness, and acceptance can break those chains. Ask Him to help you discover more powerful ways to know and apply the truth that sets us free. In prayer, meditate on one or two of the "truth statements." Speak to God:

"Lord, I take the lies captive that I have told myself for years, I confess that these false beliefs are not from You. I choose to replace these lies with Your truth and with what you want to say to me as your beloved child. I am loved, I am accepted, forgiven, chosen and belong to you. Purify my heart and mind. In Jesus name. Amen"

Week In Reveiw Questions

1. Describe the difference in Christian doctrine, practices and virtue. Why is this important to understand?

2. What does the concept of "self-awareness" mean and why is it important? Do you think many people are very self-aware, why or why not?

3. What did you learn this week concerning the importance of "self-examination" How are you learning to do healthy self-examination? What do you think about Scott Peck's quote, especially the concept of growing in our ability to be more comfortable with discomfort?

4. This week we looked at how "misbeliefs" are part of our spiritual battle. What were some of your misbeliefs?

5. What are the "Truth Statements" and Scriptures that you need to learn as a way of defeating the lies and patterns of this world?

6. Was the **ABCDE** method helpful or hard to use? Can you think of a simple way to apply what is at the heart of this exercise?

Week 5

This week is where our Strategy comes into full view. There are three fundamental habits or disciplines that define our strategy for a healthy spiritual life: Connecting to God personally, Growing with others in community, and Serving with others in life. Each of these represent a simple focus and yet, they are multifaceted and have great depth.

As we unpack the layers of Connect, Grow, and Serve, you will recognize many things you're already be doing and see others as new ways to reinforce your love and commitment to Christ. This week we will look closely at the first two: Connect and Grow; and see how our Vision is tied into our strategy.

Connect, Grow, Serve

Today, we look more closely at our actual strategy of Connect, Grow, Serve. Our strategy provides a plan to employ the spiritual disciplines as they assist us toward greater Christ-likeness. As an overview, I have arranged a list of core disciplines under each of the three parts of our strategy – our cycle of spiritual growth.

Connect	Grow	Serve
Bible engagement	Accountability	Spiritual Mentoring
Meditation	Fellowship	Discipleship
Memorization	Sharing Resources	Evangelism
Study	Hospitality	Stewardship
Worship	Encouragement	Planned Service
Prayer	Cooperate	Spontaneous Service
Gratitude	Gratitude	
Fasting	Intercession	
Petition	Confession	
Solitude/Silence	Worship	
Examination/Elimination		
Sabbath		

You do not have to engage every discipline daily, but if you are not practicing some portion of the disciplines each day your spiritual journey will suffer. Indeed, our practice of the disciplines keep our distractions to a minimum and enables us to renew our mind. Focusing on the Connect portion of our strategy, let's see how our vertical relationship with God is the greatest of all habits.

The Sponge
The way we connect and stay connected.

The sponge is an example of what happens to us when we give ourselves either to the habits of connecting to God, or to connecting with the world around us. In either case, we soak up what consumes us. If we immerse ourselves in our jobs or hobbies, we are going to talk about those things that have captured our attention. What do people love the most? Just listen to what they say.

Karen Burton Mains said it like this:
"The tongue is the indicator of the person. What we talk about all the time is what we love. The words we use and the words we don't use define what we are thinking, feeling, and becoming. We Christians must learn to undergo rigorous self-examination… if we are going to understand what we are…."

This is exactly what Jesus was saying in Luke 6:45: *"The good man brings good things out of the good stored up in his heart, and the evil man brings evil things out of the evil stored up in his heart. For out of the overflow of his heart his mouth speaks."*

Think of the sponge. What you soak up will emerge as the pressures of life squeeze you. Dallas Willard organizes the disciplines under two categories that fit well into my sponge analogy – abstinence and engagement. When we employ a discipline of abstinence we wring out our sponge. These are the disciplines of confession (admitting our sins), silence (quieting every inner and outer voice and attending to His voice), solitude (disengaging from people and things in order to attend to God) fasting (abstaining from food in order to focus on the bread of life), and examination (looking for what interferes with His word being at home in my heart).

Willard's second category of *engagement* is how we soak up God's presence. Prayer (gratitude, petition, listening, worship), and Bible engagement (reading and studying, meditation and memorization) are ways to soak in the word of God.

Jesus said in John 15:7: *"If you remain in me and my words remain in you, ask whatever you wish and it will be given to you."*

That is an invitation to be immersed in Him. To be so full of Him that the essence of who He is, the fruit of His Spirit (Ga 5:22-23) comes out of us, because He is overflowing from us. The fruit of the Spirit, indeed the power of the Spirit, isn't some mysterious thing that happens because someone prayed over you at an altar-call, or because you attended a powerful worship concert. If you are going to be known as someone who has spiritual fruit (Mt 7:16), it will be the result of soaking up God's presence and His word, aligning your heart and will to His.

On the next page, practice SOAPing Jeremiah 17:7-8. As you do, notice how this passage reinforces our sponge analogy.

Your SOAP:

_____

_____

_____

_____

_____

_____

_____

_____

_____

_____

_____

_____

_____

_____

_____

_____

_____

_____

_____

_____

_____

Connect, Grow, Serve

As a continuation of CONNECT, we now look at how our Vision connects with our strategy. Vision points to a better future. A vision is a picture on the screen of your mind that impels you forward despite obstacles. When we see clearly where we need to go, we can adjust more quickly to keep moving in that direction. A good vision is like a compass – it keeps truth North in perspective.

On Day 12 (pg. 69), we looked briefly at each of the "I am" statements. Let's quickly review. Because **"We are a loving community of growing disciples mentoring the Next Generation to live the mission of Jesus through the power of the Gospel,"** we have to know how each of us fits into that picture. Corporate change is impossible without individual change. We cannot change if I am unwilling to be a part of that change. Therefore, each of the "I am" statements gives us clarity about what has to happen in our own walk with Christ so our corporate expression of Christ can be refined.

If we are unloving, then we are going to struggle in our effort to express love as a community. If we have never been loved then we will struggle to know how to live in love. We cannot give away what we do not possess. But when we begin to experience love and grow in our understanding of what love looks like, we can aim at the same goal, encouraging one another's efforts and celebrating with each other when we hit that goal more consistently.

As you begin to meditate on each "I am" statement, you will see how each one fits directly into our strategy. The strategy (applying the disciplines through Connect, Grow and Serve) assists us in the transformational process. The catalyst for change. Renewing our mind.

"If you hold to my teaching, you really are my disciples. Then you will know the truth, and the truth will set you free." Jesus Christ

"Do not conform any longer to the pattern of this world but be transformed by the renewing of the mind." Paul, the apostle.

"Progress is impossible without change, and those who cannot change their minds cannot change anything." George Bernard Shaw

John Bradshaw in the opening of his book, *Healing the Shame that Binds You*, challenges: "The greatest problem in all of our lives is to decide and clarify our responsibility. To truly be committed to a life of honesty, love, and discipline, we must be willing to commit ourselves to reality."

If I am not cultivating my commitment to the truth (reality) God has revealed, I am likely to be living a lie. Our "I am" statements express what God says is true about who we are and what we are to be doing in this life. If I am not building my identity on God's view of me, then I am sure to be distracted by what culture says I am.

The foundation of our Vision Statement and our spiritual identity is the reality of God's view of and commitment to us. The reason we can even pursue being "a loving community" is because God, in His love has reached out for us. Consider the following passages and how without His love we have no bases or clarity on how to build our spiritual identity.

John 3:16 *"For God so loved the world that he gave his one and only Son, so that whoever believes in Him shall not perish but have everlasting life."*

Who is the lover? And who is the object of the love?

Romans 5:6-8 *"You see at just the right time, when we were still powerless, Christ died for the ungodly. Very rarely will anyone die for a righteous person, though for a good person someone might possibly dare to die. But God demonstrates his own love for us in this: while we were still sinners Christ died for us."*

Who is the initiator of love? What was the condition of the objects of that love?

1 John 3:16 *"This is how we know what love is: Jesus Christ laid down his life for us. And we also ought to lay down our lives for our brothers and sisters."*

Where do we discover what love is?

1 John 4:15-19 *"If anyone acknowledges that Jesus is the Son of God, God lives in them and they in God. And so we know and rely on the love God has for us. ...There is no fear in love. But perfect love drives out fear, because fear has to do with punishment. The one who fears is not made perfect in love. We love because he first loved us."*

How does John suggest that we become capable of love? What are the results of knowing we are loved?

The Greeks had four different words to describe the affections of love. *Eros*, a sexual bond, is where we get our word errotic. *Storge*, an empathic bond, is often used to describe the affection one person would have toward another due to familiarity, as a parent to a child. *Phileo*, is a friendship bond, which develops between comrades and is given to others freely because we like them. Lastly, *Agape*, which is an unconditional bond that was used almost exclusively by the new and burgeoning Christian community. Jesus popularized this term and used it as the distinguishing characteristic of God's love toward us and the love that would be cultivated in his followers.

Jesus made many things clear, but few topics compare with the emphasis that He placed on this new description of love.
He said in John 13:34-35: *"A new command I give you. Love one another. As I have loved you, so you must love one another. By this all men will know that you are my disciples if you love one another."*

What do you notice about the above passage and what it says about the concept of agape love?

Our first "I am" statement is the basis for the other four – "I am Loved." How does the following description of your identity in Christ move you toward God, His perspective and purposes for your life?

"I am Loved. I will focus on and celebrate that I am God's beloved child. That He loved me when I was unlovely, unworthy, and undeserving, that I might begin to see myself through His eyes. That I am a child of God; deeply loved, completely forgiven, fully pleasing and totally accepted by God, chosen by Him to reflect His love and grace. I will memorize and meditate on 1 John 4:15-19 to help me stay focused on this goal."

How is the "Connect" portion of our strategy tied to the "I am Loved" statement?
Response:

Our second "I am" statement flows right out of the first. In almost every verse above there is a response that comes out of the awareness of our being loved. We begin to love in return. That's easier said than done! Indeed it's not just the "New Commandment" it is the new life objective once we have said yes to Jesus and His presence in our lives.

We all need to be more loving. But how many of us are taking intentional, daily steps toward that end? Let's look at our "I am Loving" statement and see how it can help us to move toward a common definition of, and strategy for, love.

"I am Loving: I will work to eliminate whatever distractions are in my life and schedule that interfere with me living and loving like Jesus. I will memorize and meditate on 1 Cor. 13 to help me stay focused on that goal."

There are three things that stand out about this statement:

1) Anything that distracts us from loving needs to be eliminated
2) Jesus is the consummate example of loving
3) 1 Corinthians 13 gives us a Biblical description of what love is and what love isn't.

Begin your meditation of 1 Corinthians 13. Make a list of two categories that are itemized in verses 4-7. Behaviors that define both what love is, and isn't. You could put them under the heading of "Attractions to Love" and "Distractions from Love".

ATTRACTIONS TO LOVE   DISTRACTIONS FROM LOVE

The best way to foster a greater ability to love is to know what love is, and then spend time "CONNECTING" with the One who invented it. Go back to our 1 Corinthians text and put the name of Jesus in the place where love is used. i.e. "Jesus is patient. Jesus is kind. He does not envy...etc... you get the idea.

Prayer Focus:
As you close out your time today, give thanks for the amazing example of love we have in Christ. Take a few minutes to soak up – like a sponge – the fact that you are a child of God; deeply loved, completely forgiven, fully pleasing, and totally accepted. Pray your way through 1 Corinthians 13.
A prayer like:

"Lord, it doesn't make any difference if I can speak with the tongues of men and of angels if I am not loving... teach me to be patient...etc."

Ultimately, it is my ability to connect with God consistently (through the disciplines of prayer and Bible engagement) that will mold me into the person He wants me to be. And the person He wants me to be is a more loving person.

Connect, Grow, Serve

The power of meditation and memorization.

Stepping into the Connect, Grow, Serve cycle (strategy) of spiritual life requires intentionality. Today we focus on the disciplines of meditation and memorization. I place these two disciplines side-by-side because they are tandem. Starsky and Hutch, Bonnie and Clyde, yin and yang, Dumb and Dumber, cookies and cream. You get the idea. They just go together; and in this case, they are better together. A person can do one without the other but because of what we are trying to accomplish (being more like Jesus), they reinforce one another.

I make no bones about it. I am going to do my level best to convince you that developing this discipline can benefit you greatly and can change your entire walk with Christ, increasing impact on all of those around you.

As a high schooler, I was voted "Most likely not to succeed at anything!" I was a straight-D student who could not remember a thing on any kind of exam. If you've heard my story you know the reason, but suffice it to say, I had to work on this. And like any other habit or discipline, people think I make it look easy (but I still have to practice).

Here's how I do it and here's why Meditation is the path I suggest you take. I meditate slowly, by creating a habit. There's the concept of reading slowing, contemplating, and even praying each word and phrase. The Biblical word for meditate, "hagah," is the same word Isaiah (Is 31:7) used to describe what a lion does over its prey. He chews on every meaty morsel, growling in delight as he takes in what will make him stronger, swifter, more agile. Like the lion who consumes his prey, we need to consume God's word to make us more effective and able.

Dallas Willard says: "As a pastor, teacher and counselor, I have repeatedly seen the transformation of inner and outer life that comes simply from memorization and meditation upon Scripture. I would never undertake to... guide a program of Christian education that did not involve a continuous program of memorization of the choicest passages of Scripture....Memorization is absolutely fundamental to spiritual formation. If I had to chose between all of the spiritual disciplines of the Christian life and chose only one, I would choose Bible memorization."

Chuck Swindoll encourages us: "I know of no other single practice in the Christian life more rewarding, practically speaking, than memorizing Scripture…no other single exercise pays greater spiritual dividends! Your prayer life will be strengthened. Your witnessing will be sharper and much more effective. Your attitudes and outlook will begin to change. Your mind will become alert and observant. Your confidence and assurance will be enhanced. Your faith will be solidified."

The Old Testament calls us to meditate on God's word and promises outstanding results.

"Keep this Book of the Law always on your lips; **meditate** *on it day and night, so that you may be careful to do everything written in it. Then you will be prosperous and successful."* Joshua 1:8

Jesus told his disciples that *"If you remain in me and my* **words** *remain in you, ask whatever you wish, and it will be given to you. This is to my Father's glory, that you bear much fruit, showing yourselves to be my disciples."* John 15:7

There are many folks who push back when I challenge them to practice the habit of meditation/memorization. I hear it all the time, "I can't memorize. That's what you are good at, pastor; I'm good at other things, eating ice cream." OK maybe I'm poking fun now, but it's true. Over and over, people tell me they cannot memorize, yet spout off amazing stats from the sports world, quote verbatim some classic line from a movie, or rattle off a TV or radio ad word-for-word.

The truth is, we remember what we review, what we love, and what we care about. If you really want to grow, you will begin to submit your mind to the work of meditation on God's word of truth. What you will discover is that as you recite it, you can begin to live it with greater consistency.

Meditation leads to memorization, but memorization without meditation could lead you astray. The Pharisees, religious leaders of Jesus day, were the most learned and scholarly people of the day. They could recite large sections of Scripture and yet remained self-centered and stuck in their self-obsessed ways. Meditation is always about conforming to truth, not just quoting it.

With that caution in mind, let's proceed. As you continue through this Devotional, start or finish your time with a few minutes of focusing on one of the "I am" statements/cards and passages. You could start with "I am Loved" (1 Jn 4:14-19), "I am Loving" (1 Co 13), "I am a Disciple" (Mk 8:34-35), "I am a Mentor" (De 6:6-8), or "I am a Misisonary" (Mt 28:19-20).

As you read each day, consider the following suggestions and use them to help you in your meditation. The "I am" statements and the list below are also in our Megapack. The cards with the list of "How To Meditate" suggestions are included in "What To Do With A Megapack," available at the church office, our YC App or the Information Desk.

Prayer Focus:
Your ability to "Connect" with God will be richly blessed as you practice the habit of meditation/memorization. Take a moment and thank God for His word. We all want to hear God more effectively. The best way to hear God's voice in the future is to soak up what He has already said in the Bible. Ask God for patience to slow down and meditate on His powerful, personal word to you.

Connect, Grow, Serve

The Connect portion of our strategy is our first priority. Jesus made this point when asked about the greatest commandment in Mark 12:30-31:

"Love the Lord your God with all your heart, and with all your soul, and with all your mind, and with all your strength. This is the first and greatest commandment and the second is like it, love your neighbor as yourself."

Once we understand our first priority, loving God above all things, we can more effectively incorporate our second priority of loving others. This second commandment from Jesus moves us to the next third of our cycle of spiritual growth – GROW. The first command speaks about our vertical relationship with God; the second addresses our horizontal relationship with others. This second collection of age-old spiritual disciplines involves our engagement with others to create a loving, spiritual community.

The Early Church was quick to establish several spiritual habits that strengthened their passion for Christ, one another and God's purposes. Look at the way they are described in the second chapter of Acts:

"They devoted themselves to the apostles teaching and to the fellowship, to breaking bread and to prayer….Every day they continued to meet together in the temple courts. They broke bread together in their homes and ate together with glad and sincere hearts."

Notice the habits that they formed. They studied the apostles' teaching (Bible engagement within community). They had "fellowship" (meeting to encouragement and support one another). They ate together in homes (they did life together); and prayed (gratitude, confession, intercession and worship).

These classic Spiritual disciplines under the heading of GROW are all about doing life together. Joining a small group is the first step to cultivate these disciplines. Many of the individual disciplines under "Connect" can and should be experienced within community. Let's look again at the list that we introduced on Day 21.

GROW
Accountability
Fellowship
Mentorship/having or being a spiritual coach
Generosity/Sharing resources
Hospitality/meeting in homes
Encouragement
Cooperate
Gratitude
Intercession
Confession
Worship

The Grow Disciplines of our strategy make it clear that we are not intended to live in isolation. Go through the above list of disciplines and circle the ones that you are currently doing. Then look at those that are weak or nonexistent for you. In the space below write 2 or 3 disciplines that you are willing to try and practice. Write down when, and where, and with whom you could start. Remember that we do them "in community." We learn from one another how to practice the disciplines; how to cultivate spiritual habits that reinforce our spiritual identity.

MY PLAN:
Add the following disciplines to my routine:

1.   When   Where   With

2.   When   Where   With

3.   When   Where   With

What issues can cause someone to procrastinate or avoid this kind of application/implementation of the Grow disciplines?

Spiritual habits flow out of spiritual commitment.

As the Early Church grew, evidence of their commitment to be in community (do life together) was seen in the "one another" commands. There are 59 passages in the New Testament that use the phrase "one another." That volume alone should tell us the importance of our horizontal relationships. What follows is a brief listing that reinforces the habits of healthy community and spiritual growth:

Love.

About one third of them instruct the believer how to love one another.
– Love one another (Jn 13:34, 15:12, 17; Ro 13:8; 1 Th 3:12, 4:9; 1 Pe 1:22; 1 Jn 3:11, 4:7, 11; 2 Jn 5)
– Through love, serve one another (Ga 5:13)
– Tolerate one another in love (Ep 4:2)
– Greet one another with a kiss of love (1 Pe 5:14)
– Be devoted to one another in love (Ro 12:10)
– Humility. About 15% emphasize an attitude of humility and deference among believers.
– Give preference to one another in honor (Ro 12:10)
– Regard one another as more important than yourselves (Ph 2:3)
– Serve one another (Ga 5:13)
– Wash one another's feet (Jn 13:14)
– Don't be haughty; be of the same mind (Ro 12:16)
– Be subject to one another (Ep 5:21)
– Clothe yourselves in humility toward one another (1 Pe 5:5)

Unity.

About one third could fit under the effort that we should give toward unity.
– Be at peace with one another (Mk 9:50)
– Don't grumble among one another (Jn 6:43)
– Be of the same mind (or honor) one another (Ro 12:16, 15:5)
– Accept one another (Ro 15:7)
– Wait for one another before partaking in the Eucharist (Communion) (1 Co 11:33)
– Don't bite, devour, and consume one another – seriously, guys, don't eat each other (Ga 5:15)
– Don't boastfully challenge or envy one another (Ga 5:26)
– Gently, patiently tolerate one another (Ep 4:2)
– Be kind, tenderhearted, and forgiving of one another (Ep 4:32)
– Bear with and forgive one another (Co 3:13)
– Seek good for one another, and don't repay evil for evil (1 Th 5:15)
– Don't complain about one another (Ja 4:11, 5:9)
– Confess sins to one another (Ja 5:16)

The rest can be seen as what it takes to "do life together:"
– Do not judge one another, and don't place a stumbling block in a
 brother's way (Ro 14:13)
– Greet one another with a kiss (Ro 16:16; 1 Co 16:20; 2 Co 13:12)
– Husbands and wives, don't deprive one another of physical intimacy
 (1 Co 7:5)
– Bear one another's burdens (Ga 6:2)
– Speak truth to one another (Ep 4:25)
– Don't lie to one another (Co 3:9)
– Comfort one another concerning the resurrection (1 Th 4:18)
– Encourage and build up one another (1 Th 5:11)
– Stimulate one another to love and good deeds (He 10:24)
– Pray for one another (Ja 5:16)
– Be hospitable to one another (1 Pe 4:9)

Prayer Focus:
Write out a prayer today that confronts any personal excuse not to
follow through with your commitment to Grow within community.

Connect, Grow, Serve

Yesterday we briefly looked at the "One another" passages in the New Testament. The prolific use of this very common little phrase makes it blatantly clear that the "Growth" we need is stimulated by spending time together. We need to recognize that it's not just about being around others; we change when we are together. 1 Corinthians 15:33 reminds us that *"Bad company corrupts good character."* So it's not just being with others but how we participate in healthy community that actually refines our walk with Christ.

It's easy to fall into all kinds of behavior that disrupts healthy community. In fact, much of our New Testament instruction is about "throwing off" (getting rid of) the attitudes and behaviors that kill, steal and destroy (Jn 10:10). In Galatians 5:15 Paul says: *"If you keep on biting and devouring each other watch out or you will be destroyed by each other."* Notice how his list of things to overcome in Colossians 3:5-11 are all about improving our interaction with one another:

"Put to death, therefore, whatever belongs to your earthly nature: sexual immorality, impurity, lust, evil desires and greed, which is idolatry....You used to walk in these ways in the life you once lived but now you must rid yourselves of all such things as these, anger, rage. malice, slander and filthy language from your lips. Do not lie to one another since you have taken off your old self with its practices."

This might be a challenging exercise, but I want to press you to try this. Look back over Paul's list and write out how each behavior disrupts healthy community. For example,

  • "sexual immorality" – when sexual violation happens, at any level, there is a break of trust. (OK, now you try. Go down the list and write how each behavior affects others. Consider consulting the dictionary to give you greater insight).

  • "impurity" –

  • "lust" –

  • "evil desires" –

- "greed" –

- "anger" –

- "rage" –

- "malice" –

- "slander" –

- "filthy language" –

- "lying to one another" –

OK, now let's see how Paul replaces these behaviors. Colossians 3:12 continues with: *"Therefore, as God's chosen people, clothe yourselves (notice the analogy of taking off one set of behaviors – like dirty clothes – and putting on another set of behaviors) with compassion, kindness, humility, gentleness, and patience. Bear with each other and forgive whatever grievances you may have against one another, just as in Christ, God forgave you. And over all these virtues put on love, which binds them all together in perfect unity."*

Describe how each of these behaviors or virtues builds up and strengthens community.

- "compassion" –

- "kindness" –

- "humility" –

- "gentleness" –

- "patience" –

- "bear with each other" –

- forgive one another" –

- "love" –

Community is impossible without being with others. Learning to feel for each other and responding in ways that communicate care, concern and affection for one another is not something we do naturally; we must practice these behaviors or we will never master them.

A few days ago I compared the concepts of Christian *doctrine* (what we believe), Christian *virtue* (what we are becoming) and Christian *disciplines* (what we do or practice). What we need to become (compassionate, kind, patient) happens by practicing the spiritual disciplines, not by believing more doctrine.

Looking back at our list of spiritual disciplines under "Grow" (Day 24, pg. 129), here's how it looks. When we practice fellowship and hospitality (opening our homes and lives to each other), it causes us to face our sinful nature by choosing to give instead of get, to listen instead of talk, to share instead of hoard. When we practice confession, we confront our sinful nature (compulsion toward lust, envy, greed or any other vice) and refuse to allow it to thrive in secrecy. When we bring it into the light of loving community, we learn to be humble, compassionate, kind and forgiving. When we practice accountability, we submit a vulnerable area of our lives in order to create movement and growth where we would otherwise remain stuck. These new habits facilitate the life of the Spirit within us. By doing them, we learn to take off the old life and put on the new life. We become a new creation.

Look over your "My Plan" from yesterday and refine it based on what we considered today. Is there any discipline that you want to add or change?

MY PLAN: Add the following disciplines to my routine:
1.   When   Where   With

2.   When   Where   With

3.   When   Where   With

Prayer Focus:
Write out a prayer of confession. Look over the Colossians list of behaviors that we are called to "take off" or "get rid of." Write out a confession that can help you to eliminate some area of vulnerability in your life.

Week In Reveiw Questions

1. How does the analogy of the sponge illustrate the concept and truth of spiritual disciplines? How do you see this illustrated in your own life?

2. Can you describe our "Strategy" for spiritual development and what each part of the strategy means?

3. Why do you think our spiritual identity is so fragile, and how are the disciplines important for developing an identity based on what God says instead of what the world says?

4. How would you make a case for the importance of Scripture meditation and memorization?

5. What does it mean to die to our flesh (ego, self-will) and how are you seeking to do this? If you were to explain this concept to a junior higher, what would you say?

6. Explain why the Grow portion of our strategy is so critical. What disciplines fit into Grow?

7. How do the Grow disciplines help us to take off old behavior and put on the new behavior that reflects our commitment to Christ (Day 24 on pg 129)?

Week 6

This week we will step into the third part of our strategy, SERVE. As we do so, we will look at one condition and four expressions of what service is all about. This area, when it isn't flowing out of a strong daily connection to Jesus and tied into a humble growing community of believers, can easily begin to sour. My prayer is that this week you will recognize how important it is to not let your service for Jesus distract you from the time you need to spend with Jesus and a loving community of believers. When these first two are present, your service will be sure to shine.

Connect, Grow, Serve

I hope you are beginning to see that our Vision "Being a loving community of growing disciples mentoring the Next Generation to live the mission of Jesus through the power of the gospel" flows out of our strategy to "Connect, Grow, and Serve."

By practicing these new habits, we create a loving community of growing disciples, mentoring the Next Generation, to live the mission of Jesus, through the power of the gospel.

Today we turn our focus to the last third of our cycle of spiritual growth – SERVE. Service is where the rubber meets the road. When we decide to become followers of Christ, we have to recognize that following Jesus without serving is like wanting to fly but refusing to board a plane, wanting to run a marathon but being unwilling to jog regularly. For the next several days, we will look closely at one critical condition and four practical expressions of the Serve strategy.

Jesus gave and modeled for us the singular condition that prepares us for a life that reflects Christ. He said it this way: *"Whoever wants to become great among you must be your servant, and whoever wants to be first must be the slave of all. For even the Son of Man did not come to be served but to serve and give his life as a ransom for many."* Greatness in God's kingdom is not about what we *get*, but what we *give*. This internal condition has to be both desired and developed.

Early American settler, Briant S. Hinkley, described this singular condition as a virtue: "Service is the virtue that distinguishes the great of all time and which they will be remembered by. It places a mark of nobility on its disciples; it is the dividing line that separate the two great groups of the world. Those who help and those who hinder, those who lift and those who lean, those who contribute and those who only consume. How much better it is to give than to receive. Service in any form is comely and beautiful; to give encouragement, to impart sympathy, to show interest, to banish fear, to build self-confidence and to awaken hope in the hearts of others. In short, to love them and show it, is to render the most precious serve."

We can serve in countless ways, but service with a bad attitude doesn't count in the long run. Paul said: *"If I speak in the tongues of men and of angels but have not love I am only a resounding gong or a clanging symbol. If I have the gift of prophecy and can fathom all mysteries, and if I have a knowledge that can move mountains but have not love I am nothing. If I give all I possess to the poor and surrender my body to the flames yet have not love I gain nothing."* (1 Co 13:1-3)

Philippians 2:5 says: *"Your attitude should be the same as that of Christ Jesus who being in very nature God did not consider equality with God something to be grasped but made himself nothing taking the very nature of a servant…"*

Viktor Frankl said: "Everything can be taken from a man but one thing: the last of human freedoms – to choose one's attitude in any given set of circumstances."

How can you tell when your attitude is askew? Is your self-awareness honest enough to recognize when you are sliding toward a poor attitude? Are you able to acknowledge when your commitment to be loving is evaporating in the heat of a difficult situation? Here is a beautiful fact: *God is unreservedly committed to help you develop a better attitude, and a stronger ability to love in all circumstances.* This truth is at the core of our spiritual development and journey. Our task is to refine our personal discernment so we can quickly recognize our aberrant attitudes and surrender them to Christ, who can replace them with the heart of a servant. Definitely easier said than done!

When we practice the disciplines consistently, we learn to match our doing with our being, refining our character. The first two thirds of our cycle of spiritual life, Connect and Grow, provide the tools to increase our ability to choose our attitude in any given circumstance. Viktor Frankl said: "Between stimulus and response, there is a space. In that space lies our freedom and power to choose our response. In our response lies our growth and freedom."

Answer the following questions and complete the next exercise with your small group, close friend, or mentor:

What do you normally do when your attitude is askew?

How have you responded when someone has pointed out that you seem to be moody, cranky, irritated or just "off"?

Is there any pattern in your thought-life that might contribute to being less than loving when you struggle to adjust your attitude?

Suggested exercise: (This may be done during a group session with the "Week in Review" material)

Ask the following question to a few people close to you: "What is it like to be on the other side of me?" Press them to be completely honest. Brace yourself because you might feel your attitude or emotions souring if you don't like what you hear. This is about gaining greater self- awareness and objectivity. We have to be open to hearing how we come across if we are going to effectively refine our attitude.

On the next page, journal (record) what this exercise was like and how you think it might help you to learn.

Prayer Focus:
Write a prayer asking the Lord to develop deeper awareness within you and cultivate an attitude of service. Ask Him to fill you with an increasing desire to have a heart like His. Review today's Scripture references and add some new insight to your prayer.

Your Journal entry:

_____

_____

_____

_____

_____

_____

_____

_____

_____

_____

_____

_____

_____

_____

_____

_____

_____

_____

_____

_____

_____

Serve

Yesterday we introduced the third piece of our strategy – SERVE and covered the condition for SERVICE – serving from a heart (or attitude) that is being transformed by Christ's presence. Today we look at the four expressions of service that will illustrate our commitment to know Christ and make Him known.

The dictionary defines SERVE: "to furnish or supply with something needed or desired." Let's gain clarity on our own personal responsibility to respond to the call to Biblical servanthood. Answer the question: "Are there certain things we are all called to do as believers that are expressions of Christ's presence in us?"

The condition we considered yesterday is the first critical piece of any act of service – the heart (or attitude) we bring to what we do for Christ. One of my favorite Scriptures (for the purpose for Bible engagement-meditation and memorization, making truth more accessible to your consciousness) is Colossians 3:23-24: *"Whatever you do, work at it with all your heart, as working for the Lord, not for men, since you know that you will receive an inheritance from the Lord as a reward. It is the Lord Christ you are serving."*

Write a short statement about what this passage says about the "condition" our heart needs to be in for healthy service to take place.

The four expressions are: Mentoring (or discipling), Being a missionary (sharing our faith with those far from God), Using our giftedness for Him as a functioning part of the body of Christ (where the great diversity to our serving falls) and Spontaneous service (serving as needed).

Imagine that you have been hired to work for a company that has an amazing reputation. You are excited because this company has been around for what feels like forever. They have the best service record of any company you know, have amazing employee benefits and an unbelievable retirement plan. On your first day, all new employees (they are constantly adding new partners-everyone gets shares right off the bat) are brought into a lovely room and instructed on several key employee responsibilities.

The CEO himself is there (everyone loves this guy because he personifies a servant's heart). As everyone arrived, he was out front greeting each person with a welcoming hug and warm handshake. It seemed as if he touched you; part of himself added something good to your life.

As he begins to speak, everyone eagerly gives him their complete attention. He clarifies that there are four categories of service, but there is one area that supersedes all of what we do. That is, how we do what we do. He explains that if we can keep this first thing first, everything else (these other four areas) will fall nicely into place." Everyone is on the edge of their seats as he continues: "This first skill can help you master everything else. It is your power to choose the right attitude in any given circumstance. It is the choice to be loving, to be patient and kind regardless of the challenge or task in front of you."

He goes on to explain that when the right attitude is present, every other task can be transformed into an expression of goodness, teamwork and integrity.

He shares that he learned this important skill from his father. He explains that when he serves from this place (attitude) of gratefulness and passion, he senses his father's presence flowing through his words and acts of service.

"Now," he says, "let's look closely at the four expressions where this attitude can shine through us. The first two are areas that all of us are responsible for, and the other two are as unique as each individual."

"The first two are all about relationships – our relationship with those who are new to the company, and those who are strangers to the good things we have to offer. You see, you are a coach or a mentor to someone coming up behind you, and each one an ambassador to those we want to invite into our fold." And with a smile and a wink he says, "Which is everyone, right?"

"The second two areas are unique to you. One is your unique giftedness, and the other is your unique circumstance."

With an uncanny confidence he begins to point out person after person in the room, highlighting their specific gifting (special abilities). He makes the wise, insightful point that our abilities and gifts are exactly what we are supposed to use to fit in and contribute to the company's success. It seems to bring a peace over everyone, knowing that we have something special to offer right out of the acumen we already possess.

"When it comes to your unique circumstances," he explains, "we are able (when we are tuned in to that proper attitude) to step into a situation, a problem, or a spontaneous opportunity, and serve. The task in this scenario doesn't usually require a special ability but rather a humble availability. Suppose," he says, "you are walking into a mall and you notice that someone has fallen and stumbled over an uneven piece of sidewalk. They clearly are not bouncing right up. "What do you do?" Everyone expresses the obvious: "Well, help them up!"

"Yes!" he exclaims with a huge smile. "You see anytime you serve from the attitude of gratitude, kindness, and love, you represent us. You represent me and the commitment that we all share, to show how much we care about people."

What do you see from the allegory? Who was the CEO and what are the four expressions of service? See if you can bullet out each one with your own short description.

-

-

-

-

Which of these do you apply well, and which are almost completely off your daily radar? Do these areas of service make sense, or is there some level of confusion?

Prayer Focus:
Spend a few minutes praying about where you currently are with each of these four areas, and where you are called to reflect a heart of service.

Serve

I Am A Mentor

Let's look more closely at how mentoring is an expression of service. At the end of our study of both our Vision and our "Connect, Grow, Serve" strategies, we saw how they interface nicely. Our Vision reminds us that mentoring is who we are. When we cultivate our faith and live with intentionality, we cannot ignore that we are called to mentor (disciple) others.

> **"We are a loving community of growing disciples mentoring the Next Generation to live the mission of Jesus through the power of the gospel."**

To own this piece of our vision and serve as mentors, we might have to reprioritize some things in our life. Simply put, following Jesus involves mentoring. Regi Campbell, in his book, *Mentor Like Jesus*, says: "Jesus was a mentor. Those He mentored totally committed to His mission, and worked together as an effective team."

The primary reason for mentoring is because Jesus modeled this method for us. Discipleship, at its most basic level, pairs relationships that foster a greater dependence on God, a deeper trust in one another, and an intentional accountability which moves both parties further along in their faith journey.

Tim Elmor, President of Growing Leaders, discusses a principle that affirms why we should pursue the commitment to be a mentor: "More time spent with fewer people equals greater kingdom impact." It's what Jesus did!

Read through our definition of what a mentor does, and evaluate your own walk with Christ and preparedness for mentoring. If we have not established our identity in Christ, it will be hijacked by culture. Using the mentoring definition, notice the progression that is necessary to have a mature view of who we are in God's eyes.

To mentor: "to help or assist another to discover, establish and refine their spiritual identity."

When we know who we are in Christ, we are much less distracted by the culture around us. When the children of Israel were delivered from bondage in Egypt they struggled to shed their identity as slaves. It has been said that it took one night to get the Israelites out of Egypt, but 40 years to get Egypt out of Israel. Romans 6 states that we are slaves to whatever controls us. Just as God helped the Israelites to adopt a new spiritual identity (Ex 19:5-6) so we must work to embrace our new identity in Christ. This is one of our most fundamental tasks of spiritual growth in ourselves and with those we mentor. We cannot give away what we do not possess.

Looking closely at the above definition, answer the following: How can you strengthen your own spiritual identity?

When did you accept Christ as your Savior or "discover" your spiritual identity? Do you remember the month and year, and what were the circumstances that brought you into a relationship with Jesus?

How "well established" is your own faith in Christ (your identity), and why? What would you say would be markers of an established faith?

According to Deuteronomy 6:6-8, what is unique about the form of teaching/training that is suggested? What would you say is the "big idea" of this passage?

Our "I am a Mentor" statement helps us to move ourselves toward greater obedience to fulfill this expression of service.

"I will seek to be an example that anyone can follow, an observational mentor to all of the youth in my sphere of influence and an intentional mentor to a few. I will memorize and meditate on Deuteronomy 6:6-9 and Philippians 4:9 to help me stay focused on this goal."

Continue to process with a few others these important steps to become an intentional mentor.

1. Look at each of the three degrees for mentoring. Which one best describes your current connection to the next generation? Are you an unintentional mentor (an example with no real awareness of who is watching), an observational mentor (paying close attention to the youth around you and trying to speak into their lives with care and encouragement), or an intentional mentor (having identified a young person with whom you spend committed time for the purpose of developing their spiritual identity)?

2. Think of your own life and those who have had some level of spiritual influence on you. Try to put a name to each of these degrees:

- Who has been an unintentional role model for you?

- Who has spoken consistently into your life in a positive way and helped you believe they personally cared, and assisted you in some life skill?

- And who, if anyone, have you intentionally and consistently met with for the purpose of your growth and development? From what I have observed and read, this is often a very small category.

3. Zero in on who you could mentor. Before Jesus selected the 12 disciples (those He would mentor over the next three years), He spent time in prayer. I want to invite you to pray and ask God to show you that particular young person in your sphere of influence. Make a list of the 20-somethings (or younger) that you are around regularly. Nieces, nephews, grandchildren, neighbors, coworkers or their kids, etc. Once you have a potential mentee in mind, muster up the courage to ask if they would be open to meeting with you weekly to pursue a deeper connection to Jesus.

A word of caution. When it comes to intentional mentoring stay with the same sex. We are called to live above reproach. Consider other men and women to refer and connect the young person you care about to another committed believer of the same sex.

Prayer Focus:
Close your time today praying and asking God to show you someone to mentor. This might take time. Be determined and ask others in your small group or your own mentor to hold you accountable.

Look in the appendix for a detailed outline of our strategy for mentoring.

Serve

I Am A Missionary

Being a missionary is the second area where we are all called to serve. Sharing our faith with those who have not made a commitment to Christ is as clear in Scripture as any of Jesus' commands and yet is one of the most neglected. The result is that most believers are reluctant at best, and adverse at worst, to obeying the call to give away what we have freely been given. The famous preacher from the late 1800's, Charles Spurgeon, said it as bluntly as I have heard it: "As a Christian, you are either a missionary or an imposter."

I will be the first to confess that I have struggled to be obedient to this aspect of our faith. I know, from personal angst, just how intimidating it can be to share with someone far from God. It seems like we can fluctuate from mild discomfort to utter terror at the thought. Surely it doesn't have to be so difficult.

Writing it into our Vision statement and strategy illustrates my resolve to do my best to fix this great neglect and better equip those under my care to serve God's kingdom by growing in our commitment to reach out to those who do not know Him. Wasn't this the purpose of Christ's coming?

Jesus said *"The Spirit of the Lord is on me, because he has anointed me to preach the good news to the poor. He has sent me to proclaim freedom for the prisoners and recovery of sight for the blind, to release the oppressed, to proclaim the year of the Lord's favor."* Luke 4:18-19

I am convinced that being a mentor and a missionary do not come naturally or easily. This is why we have to recognize that they are as much a part of the spiritual disciplines as prayer and Bible engagement. If you are waiting for it to just happen it won't. A neat and tidy home isn't something that pops into existence. If you are waiting for your house to get clean or your lawn to be mowed, you'll soon be swimming in dirty dishes and standing in knee-high grass. If we want to share God's love and plan for salvation and eternal life, we'll have to engage the steps to get there. Otherwise we will only be recipients of His salvation instead of the ambassadors that He seeks (2 Co 5:20). Look up 2 Corinthians 5:18-21 and write out what it says about who we are to be and what we are to be doing in response to what Christ has done for us.

2 Corinthians 5:18-21

When Paul uses the term "ambassadors," he is describing us as missionaries. This is a part of our new spiritual identity. To change the way we see ourselves, we have to recognize that we have to be willing to embrace a different picture of who we are.

That happens all the time when a person is hired into a new job or position in a company. If you were hired as a clerk, receptionist, or sales person, you would automatically be called upon to represent the organization that employs you. Most employers are going to feel strongly about what kind of representative you are. If you enjoy your new position and if you are grateful for the company (liking its mission and values), then you are much more likely to be internally motivated to be a good representative. With many positions, an employee literally will put on a new identity to fulfill their new responsibilities. This will often include a uniform and a name-tag, designating the role the employee fills. With a similar metaphor, Scripture says that when we accept a relationship with Christ, we are given a new identity, a new name and a new responsibility as representatives of Christ. Reveiw each of the following passages and answer the question: "What is the metaphor in each passage and what is the new responsibility?"

1 Corinthians 6:19-20

1 Peter 2:9-12

Colossians 3:12-17

Three things are critical for us to see with this new God-given identity. The disciples followed a very simple, yet profound process that moved them into the realm of God's kingdom purposes: observation, imitation, repetition. They watched what Jesus did, they imitated His behavior by following His example, and repeated the process over and over.

First is the process of *observation* – we have to catch a vision for being a disciple, a mentor and a missionary. Jesus cast the vision of the Great Commission from the get-go. Literally, His first invitation to the fishermen by the Sea of Galilee (Mk 1) was accompanied by the future notion of fishing for men, morphing their earthly identity with a new spiritual identity. When we begin to see what Jesus wants to do in us and through us, we can align ourselves with His will, instead of trying to manipulate Him to our will. Just seeing His will does not mean we will do it or do it well, but it does clarify where we need to be headed.

Second, they were *imitators* of Christ – they followed Christ's example. Paul said in 1 Corinthians 11:1: *"Be imitators of me, just as I am of Christ."* I love how Matthew 11:29 (MSG) reads: *"...walk with me, work with me, watch how I do it, learn the unforced rhythms of grace."* Just because we make a commitment doesn't mean we will become competent. We have to learn new skills, disciplines and habits to become proficient at any important task.

Third, the disciples practiced *repetition*. Numerous times, they put into practice what they observed and were taught. We cannot learn anything well without repetition. Only then do we become confident in living out our faith. That is the result of discipline and self-control. Hebrews 12:11b (MSG) says this about being a disciple: *"... it is the well-trained who find themselves mature in their relationship with God."*

So where are you training? Where do you practice living out your faith? You can do it just about anywhere and with anyone, but if you don't decide to begin somewhere with someone, you won't develop. Our "I am a missionary" statement is simply what Scripture calls us to be with an emphasis on the motivation being Christ-centered. As you begin to think about who God has called you to be and what He has called you to do, these new thought patterns can empower you to be a much more engaged Christ follower. Over the next two days, we will learn two very critical skills to being a missionary – how to articulate the big God story and how to tell our own story of salvation in Christ. This isn't just our new job, it's our new identity.

Prayer Focus:
Tell the Lord how you feel about your new identity as a missionary. Are you eager to pick up this aspect of your God calling or is it difficult to see yourself as an ambassador? Ask Him to help you fully embrace His call on your life.

Serve

I Am A Missionary

The Great Commission: Christ's last send off to His disciples shows up in every Gospel and the book of Acts. Five times Jesus is recorded commanding His most intimate followers to make disciples (to be sent, to preach, and to be His witnesses) throughout the whole world (Mt 29:19-20; Mk 16:15; Lk 24:26-27; Jn 20:21-22 and Ac 1:8). This Command is not just for them but for us. The first Disciples died trying but the fulfillment of this command can only come as we, Jesus' current disciples, embrace His Mission.

Helping people make a decision. We cannot be a disciple, as the New Testament describes, if we are unwilling to make a decision. Our decision to follow Jesus precedes our commitment to be like Jesus. The decision to follow Jesus is the turning point where we acknowledge that our way will lead to death and His way will lead to life. We reach a point where we admit that he is God and we are not; instead of running our own life and trusting in our good deeds, we will put our trust in Him.

The whole "Gospel" story is about this turning point and its subsequent results. We call this "God's grand narrative of redemption," or the "God story." Throughout the pages of Scripture God is calling people to follow and to trust Him over everything else. When we learn how to tell our story as it fits into the God story, we find our most powerful tool for inviting others into their own relationship with Christ. We are committed to help you articulate both the God story and your own story so you will be prepared to give an answer whenever God presents an opportunity.

Spend a few minutes meditating on our "I am a Missionary" statement. In order to learn to tell the God story more effectively, write the main points from each passage on the next page.

I will obey the Great Commission as an expression of my love for Christ. I will grow in my ability and commitment to spread the message of Christ's love to those around me and around the world. I will do what I can do and support those who can do more than I can do through my faith promise. I will memorize and meditate on John 20:21, Matthew 28:19-20 and 1 Peter 3:15 to help me stay focused on this goal.

John 20:21

Matthew 28:19-20

1 Peter 3:15

One of the most difficult nuances of our sinful nature to recognize and dispel is our compulsion to think that life is all about us. Our narcissistic culture encourages to do whatever we want in our personal pursuit of happiness. It's the American way. Life, liberty and the pursuit of happiness. We want to be the star in our own story. This can sound rather innocent, even affirming. As individuals pursue a life driven by personal lusts, it's not uncommon to hear comments like. "You go boy, do your own thing," or "Hey, she deserves to be happy."

The great deception of Satan is that we can be happy by ignoring God and focusing obsessively on ourselves. Michael Horton in his book, *The Gospel Driven Life* says, "Repentance means I give up my script; I stop pretending that I can write the story of my life. Through faith in Christ, I become a character in God's story, part of the new creation."

To understand how we fit into God's story we must first realize that God is always at work. I might not know exactly what He is doing, but the better I know Him the more likely I can recognize His activity. For instance, God always wants to make Himself known. This can come through verbal or nonverbal witness. In fact, God always wants believers to be "light" to a dark world (Mt 5:14-16).

When we practice the Spiritual disciplines, we learn to tune into the Spirit and become more aware of God's agenda. This is important because when I am in tune with Him (walking in the Spirit), I will readily see the opportunities before me.

Consider Colossians 4:2-6 in light of God's desire to be known through us as missionaries.

"Devote yourselves to prayer, being watchful and thankful. And pray for us, too, that God may open a door for our message, so that we may proclaim the mystery of Christ, for which I am in chains. Pray that I may proclaim it clearly, as I should. Be wise in the way you act toward outsiders; make the most of every opportunity. Let your conversation be always full of grace, seasoned with salt, so that you may know how to answer everyone."
What stands out to you?

God wants to open doors for us to engage others in God's purposes. One of the things that stands out to me from the Colossians passage is the need for "clarity". Paul says: *"Pray that I may proclaim it clearly as I should...."* Clarity is a huge part of being a Missionary/representative. In the space below, I have given you the God Story in a drawing.* Each of the (1-7) steps correspond to one of the words or steps in the drawing. This is a great picture to draw out over a conversation about God and His love for us. Using the steps below, follow along with the message and the picture it describes.

1. "Adam" the first man (in fact that's what his name means, "man") was the one who first chose to sin against God. The Bible says in Romans 5:12: *"sin entered the world through one man...."* Place "Adam" in the upper left corner. Then descend down the line with little dots signifying the generations of mankind that continue to sin. This is where you can draw the stick figure showing how each of us are following in the line of Adam. Romans 3:23 says: *"All have sinned and fall short of the glory of God."*

*I have modified this image slightly from the SALT material produced by Victorious Christian Living International.

2. This leads to spiritual "death." Write "Death" at the bottom of the line in the lower right hand corner. Proverbs says "There is a way that seems to be right to a man, but in the end it leads to death."

3. Next draw a horizontal line and write the word "Righteous" or "Just" on the left side of the line that goes across the page. God is "Just "and he is "Righteous". His standards do not change, and because he is "Just" we remain accountable for sins. Write the word "Eternal"on the opposite end of the horizontal line. Because God is eternal and He wants us (the objects of His love) to experience eternal life.

We live in a world that believes in a "Justice system" where those who break laws are to be held accountable for their violation. This concept is a part of God's story throughout history. God says that we can never meet His standard completely, therefore He sent Jesus, the perfect man, to be the payment for sin, to take our place, so justice can be served (Ro 3:21-26). The word Righteous means "Right standing" therefore, if someone keeps all the laws, they are in right standing with the justice system.

4. Now draw the cross just to the left of the stick person who represents each of us (we are all on this downward spiral toward death and separation from God). John 3:16 says: *"God so loved the world that he gave his son, so that whoever believes on him shall have eternal life."*

5. Now draw an arrow from the stick figure to the cross and write the words, "Our part" above the arrow and the word "Believe" below the arrow. Romans 10:9 says, *"If you confess with your mouth that Jesus is Lord, and believe in your heart that God raised him from the dead, you will be saved."* That's our part.

6. Now draw a big arch arrow from the stick figure over to the horizontal line and draw another stick figure on the line. This represents that we are now in "right standing with God." Romans 1:16 &17 says, *"A righteousness (right standing) from God is revealed, that is by faith (believing)..."* When we believe in and accept a relationship with Christ (God's ultimate expression of redemption) he "justifies" us, puts us in right standing with him.

7. Now, over the arch arrow write the words, "God's Part." Romans 5:1 says: *"Therefore, since we have been justified through faith, we have peace with God through our Lord Jesus Christ, through whom we have gained access by faith into this grace in which we now stand."*

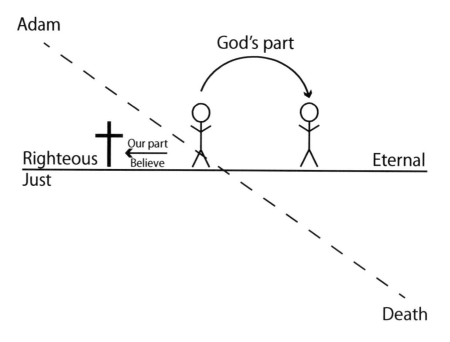

This is a powerful resource to help you bring clarity to the God Story. With a little practice you can share this effective picture of the Big God Story and how we can enter into an eternal relationship with God. Practice with a friend, mentor or small group. If you want to watch me draw out the illustration check it out on our YC app.

Prayer Focus:
This is a great place to exercise the discipline of gratitude. Simply express your gratitude for salvation; for being put in "right standing" before God because of Jesus and His paying the debt of our sin. Ask the Lord to open a door for you to tell the God Story more clearly.

Week In Reveiw Questions

1. Review the Viktor Frankl quotes (pg. 143) about our ability to choose our attitude. What happens between "stimulus and response?" How are you learning to navigate yourself out of a bad attitude? How is that working?

2. Ask a few close friends: "What is it like to be on the other side of me?" Press them to be completely honest. Brace yourself because you may feel your attitude or emotions souring if you don't like what you hear.

3. Can you articulate the one condition and four expressions of service? What stood out to you from the allegory of the CEO and impressive service company?

4. Where are you with the goal to become a mentor? Just beginning to think about it, have been mentored and now want to become a mentor, or you are currently doing intentional mentoring? What would be your next step?

5. From the material on being a missionary, do you consider yourself a missionary? Why or why not? What does the 1 Peter 3:15-16 passage present as our responsibility?

6. Can you draw the big God Story and tell how we are able to come into "right standing" with God? Ask if someone in your small group can draw the diagram.

Week 7

This week you will start to write your personal story of how you came to Christ. This is a strategic step to gain more confidence in sharing your faith. Your story is special, unique and when told well extremely powerful. I hope I get to hear your story. Once you have written it please pull me aside to share it with me.

This week we will also look at several areas that I've called "Healthy Boundaries" Money, sex and time. Many of the things that go wrong in relationship; families, businesses and churches fall into one of these categories. Learning to set good boundaries can powerfully reinforce our commitment to live out a life that honors Christ.

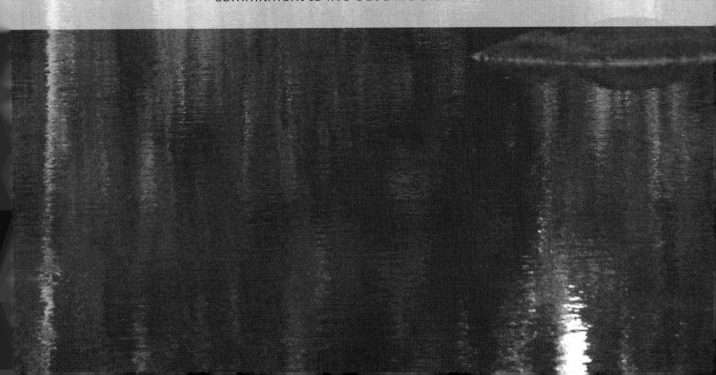

Standards For Healthy Discipleship

Write Your Story

If you have accepted a relationship with Christ and have affirmed Him as Lord and Savior, then you have a faith story. This is where your and intersects with God's grand narrative. One of our goals under this calling to tell God's story (being a Missionary) is to be able to confidently tell our own God story, how we came to place our trust in Him (when we discovered our spiritual identity). Today, let's take a first step in that direction. Under each of the following points write out your own story. It's OK to struggle, just do your best and then ask your mentor, small group leader or one of our staff to help you. As you prepare to give an answer, you will be amazed at the opportunities that begin to come your way.

On the next page, follow the guidelines below and write out your first draft of "Your Story"*.

Your Life Before Christ: Paint a picture of what your life was like before Christ (but don't dwell too heavily on how bad it was or glory in past sin). Share only the details that relate to how you were lost, misled or confused spiritually.

How you came to Christ: Make sure to speak in a clear way so that those who hears you can understand how you became a Christian and how they can become a Christian too.

Prayer: Insert the simple prayer that you said to ask Jesus into your heart. Something like:

"Lord Jesus, I know that I am a sinner and I ask for Your forgiveness. I believe that You died for my sins and rose from the dead. I turn the leadership of my life over to You. I invite You to come into my heart and life. I ask you to be my Lord and Savior. In Jesus' name, Amen."

Your Life After Christ: Share some of the changes that Christ has made in your life as they relate to your life and story. Emphasize the changes in your character, attitude and perspective, not just the changes in your behavior. And be realistic. We will struggle as Christians. Life isn't perfect, but what makes it different for you now? Be honest and God will use your personal experience regardless of how unspectacular you think it is.

* Taken from the Billy Graham "My Hope America" taining material.

Closing: You can wrap up the story with a favorite Scripture (that relates to your story) or a statement that ties your story together. Once your first draft is complete, identify a thread – what did your life revolve around that helped bring you to Him (For me it was a learning disorder that fueled my insecurities and fears)? If you can find a thread, you can take the first step to refine your story.

Once you finish the first draft, sit with a mentor or your small group or even one of the church staff to get input about how to continue to refine your story. This is a big deal. You will be much more empowered to give an answer (especially a clear one) when you're prepared. Whitney Young, Jr said: "I would rather be prepared for an opportunity and not have one then to have an opportunity and not be prepared."

Prayer Focus:
Ask the Lord to help you to articulate your story well. Look for open doors, then tell your story (to give an answer) about how you have been caught up in the story of God.

First Draft:

_____

_____

_____

_____

_____

_____

_____

_____

_____

_____

_____

_____

_____

_____

_____

_____

_____

_____

_____

_____

_____

First Draft:

_____

_____

_____

_____

_____

_____

_____

_____

_____

_____

_____

_____

_____

_____

_____

_____

_____

_____

_____

_____

_____

Second Draft:

_____

_____

_____

_____

_____

_____

_____

_____

_____

_____

_____

_____

_____

_____

_____

_____

_____

_____

_____

_____

_____

Second Draft:

_____

_____

_____

_____

_____

_____

_____

_____

_____

_____

_____

_____

_____

_____

_____

_____

_____

_____

_____

_____

Third Draft:

_____

_____

_____

_____

_____

_____

_____

_____

_____

_____

_____

_____

_____

_____

_____

_____

_____

_____

_____

_____

Third Draft:

_____

_____

_____

_____

_____

_____

_____

_____

_____

_____

_____

_____

_____

_____

_____

_____

_____

_____

_____

_____

Standards For Healthy Discipleship

Stewardship

A flourishing disciple has learned the balance between **concentration** and **elimination.**

To foster a culture of growing disciples, we focus on what we want to become (our vision), and also realize what distractions might be keeping us from becoming what we are called to be.

Steven Pauls says: "The place for what you want is already filled with what you've settled for instead." To successfully make room for Christ and His call on our lives, we have to concentrate on what we eliminate.

Peter Drucker calls this "knowing the value of planned abandonment." This week we look at several areas where disciples/Christ followers can easily be blindsided. Scripture tells us that Satan is crafty (Ge 3:1), a liar (Jn 8:44) and a thief (Jn 10:8), and that he is analogous to a lion looking for lunch (1 Pe 5:8). If you are not careful, you could be a snack!

The best way not to be blindsided is to know where you are vulnerable (self-awareness). We first have to recognize our vulnerability and then work to develop the skills and habits to be prepared for the inevitable attack that will come. I call these habits and skills "standards for healthy disciples." Before we dig into each area, look over the list below and circle which areas you may be most vulnerable and write a brief reason why under each topic:

- Preoccupied with material things

- Overly busy and/or mismanaged priorities

- Unresolved hurt and conflict

- Prone to gossip or misspeak

- Vulnerable to relational compromise (sexual or emotional)

Even a quick review of these five categories could cause a little anxiety. A person could easily think: "What are they trying to do here, get into my business?!?" The answer to that is both "no," and "yes." Being "real" and being "healthy" are both highly vauled characteristics, but one does not guarantee the other. Some folks are very real, but not very healthy. Jesus wants you – we want you – to be healthy, but you cannot have the latter without the former. To become a healthy disciple, I first have to be a real disciple, an honest disciple, willing to let truth into my life in order to free me from any lies that could hold me captive. We believe Jesus when He said that the "... *truth will set you free*" (Jn 8:32b). The scary thing is that the truth might first make you miserable, afraid or very anxious. This last week might be invasive, but that is what Jesus does. He invades our private world and begins to conquer our fears, hurts and points of resistance.

A steward is one who has been entrusted with the resources of another. The Bible tells us that we are stewards. We have been given our time, our giftedness, our relationships, our ability to work and produce wealth; not for our comfort, but for His cause. It belongs to God. Moses wanted the Israelites to understand this principle so in Deuteronomy 8:17-18 he challenged their self-talk by saying: *"You may say to yourself, 'My power and the strength of my hands have produced this wealth for me' But remember the Lord your God, for it is he who gives you the ability to produce wealth..."*

When it comes to our money and possessions, we engage in self-talk. We tell ourselves how hard we have worked, how much we deserve it, and how little we have compared with other people. There are all kinds of things we do to try and condone our spending and desires to have more. The problem is that material things will never satisfy, because we were not designed to find happiness in possessions. Happiness is a personal relationship with God. C.S. Lewis said it like this: "God designed the human machine to run on Himself. He Himself is the fuel our spirits were designed to burn. The food our spirits were designed to feed on. There is no other. That is why it is just no good asking God to make us happy in our own way without bothering about religion. God cannot give you a happiness and peace apart from Himself because it is not there."

The compulsion to consume is particularly evident in America. Today we consume twice the goods and services per person as we did 50 years ago, and the average home size has tripled. The term that one sociologist has given to describe our obsession with possessions is "affluenza." We've contracted the disease of materialism.

Throughout this devotional we have been looking at being more discerning of our self-talk. Are you aware of your self-talk? What do you tell yourself about what you have or don't have? Have you ever caught yourself measuring your value by your valuables? Does the cancer of comparison ever rob you of your joy? I can still remember years ago driving by a new home with a three-car garage and immediately becoming disenchanted with my home – thinking that if I were really successful, I'd possess a bigger house with a three-car garage. That was so stupid! I had to realize that my earning would probably never match my yearning. Therefore, if I was going to experience contentment, I was going to have to submit my heart and all of its desires to Him.

Scripture calls us to give and tithe (10%) as a way to maintain our focus as stewards keeping God and His purpose as a priority in our lives. Someone has appropriately asked: "If God owns it all, maybe instead of asking how much we should give, we should be asking how much we should keep."

Consider each of the following quotes and select one or two on which to write a reflection:

Billy Graham: "A checkbook is a theological document. It tells who and what you worship."

Martin Luther: "I have held many things in my hands and have lost them all; but that which I have placed in His hands, that I still possess."

Winston Churchill: "We make a living by what we get; we make a life by what we give."

Lynn Miller: "Stewardship is the act of organizing your life so that God can spend you."

Barbara Bush: "Giving frees us from the familiar territory of our own needs by opening our minds to the unexplained worlds occupied by the needs of others."

Jesus Christ: *"Where your treasure is, there your heart will be also."*

Personal Reflection 1:

Personal Reflection 2:

What do the following Scriptures teach us about stewardship? Write under each verse what it says to you about being a steward.

"The earth is the LORD's and everything in it, the world, and all who live in it." Psalm 24:1

"Remember this: Whoever sows sparingly will also reap sparingly, and whoever sows generously will also reap generously. Each man should give what he has decided in his heart to give, not reluctantly or under compulsion, for God loves a cheerful giver."
2 Corinthians 9:6-7

"Moreover it is required in stewards, that a man be found faithful."
1 Corinthians 4:2 (KJV)

"The purpose of tithing is to teach you always to put God first in your lives." Deuteronomy 14:23 (LB)

Being a giver — one who contributes — is fundamental to your faith. What are you learning about becoming someone who makes a commitment to give faithfully?

How would you now re-define "stewardship" based on today's study?

Prayer Focus:
How are you doing as a steward of your resources? Ask the Lord what He would have you give back to Him (a spiritual discipline) as a way to keep your focus on putting Him first in all that He has given you to manage.

Standards For Healthy Discipleship

Tackling Your Time

If we make time for what matters, what does your time say about the importance of your faith and relationship with Christ?

The apostle Paul told both the Ephesians and Colossians believers to make the best use of their time (Ep 5:15-16; Cl 4:5). If we are going to be effective stewards of our time, we have to evaluate how we manage it.

We do not all have the same talents, the same opportunities or the same resources; but we do have the same amount of time. What you do with your time, your 24-hour day, your 1440-minute day, makes you who you are. Today, ask yourself what kind of steward you are of your time, and then make a commitment to obey the above passages of Scripture to make the best use of your time.

Dartmouth College Professor, E. B. Osborn, said: "Besides the task of acquiring the ability to organize a day's work, all else you will ever learn about management is child's play."

In order to effectively manage your time, you need to do three things:

1) Analyze your activities: If you don't control your activities, your activities will control you. Ephesians 5:15 says: *"pay close attention to how you live. Don't live like ignorant men, but like wise men."* And Psalm 90:12 says: *"Teach us to number our days."*

2) Utilize your opportunities: The Ephesians 5 passage goes on to say, in verse 16: *"Make the most of every opportunity..."* Whitney Young, Jr., said: "I would rather be prepared for an opportunity and not have one, than to have an opportunity and not be prepared." The task of discipleship is to be disciplined with our preparation so we can be ready for any opportunities for explanation. 1 Peter 3:15 says: *"Always be prepared to give an answer to everyone who asks you to give the reason for the hope that you have..."*

3) Prioritize your responsibilities: Our Ephesians text in the Phillips translation says: *"Live life with a due sense of responsibility, not as those who do not know the meaning of life, but as those who do."*

Okay, let's start. Let's analyze first, and then we'll utilize and prioritize. Look at the following Scriptures and answer the corresponding question.

For what purpose were you created? Ephesians 2:10

What does God want you to do? Mark 10:43-45

How has God gifted you? Romans 12:3-8; 1 Peter 4:10

When we realize that God has made and gifted us to bring honor to Him, we are on the way to discovering the abundant life. When this truth becomes a reality in our lives, the ordinary becomes extraordinary. When ordinary people become zealous about the task before them, they are no longer ordinary. Martin Luther King, Jr., said:

"If a man is called to be a street sweeper, he should sweep streets even as Michelangelo painted, or Beethoven composed music, or Shakespeare wrote poetry. He should sweep streets so well that all the hosts of heaven and earth will pause to say, here lived a great street sweeper who did his job well."

Now let's look at where you are called to shine. We each have "key areas" of responsibility. Just ahead there is a worksheet to help you organize your week, one day at a time. Before you go to work organizing your time, think about the key areas of your life. For most of us, these areas are similar: your walk with God (CONNECT, GROW, & SERVE); your emotional and physical health, marriage, parenting, work, ministry, hobby, etc.

Go to the worksheet on the next page and fill in your "key areas," in order of priority. You may have 4 to 7 areas. If these areas are indeed part of your responsibility and values, then they must show up on your calendar of activities.

Once you've done this, under each "key area," write 3-4 things, or tasks, you want to be sure to include in that area (See my Work List Sample on pg 190).

There are three or four lines under each key area. Write the activities that you believe need to happen under each "key area" and then give it a letter of priority.

"A" = Something you "must do."
"B" = Something you "should do."
"C" = Something you "could do."

This will help you to recognize if you are putting what is truly important in the right place of priority. For instance, if I say that my "walk with God" is my highest priority of all my "key areas" yet not giving any of the tasks in that area an "A" or a "B", then I don't really believe I need to do it. Therefore, if I put down an "A" next to "Bible meditation," I'm saying I must do this to make my walk with God a priority. An "A", "must do," doesn't mean I will die if I don't do it; but I guarantee you, any key area will die if it is not supported by real and faithful action (discipline).

Before you drop your list of "tasks" into your calendar, think about your day in blocks of time: morning, afternoon, and evening. You may do something like a quiet time with God, every day. Other things you may do only once a week, or once a month. After you have finished your lists, transfer the most important things into the timeframe you intend to do for that week.

Here are five things to consider as you do this work:

1) *Learn to say "no."* Every time you say "no" to something, you create space for something better.

2) *Control your phone (technology) so it does not control you.* When doing an important task, or when you are with someone, make them the priority, not your phone. Schedule a block of time to return phone calls.

3) *Write it down* – Important things that we say we are going to do, or people we meet need to be documented quickly before we forget, then go back and review them or put them on your calendar.

4) *Get your rest!* Studies show that we need between 7-9 hours of sleep to function at our best. Try to be as consistent with your schedule as you can. Routine and predictability are critical steps for stability.

5) *Review your calendar* at the beginning of each month, week and day to always keep your focus on what matters most.

Prayer Focus:
Lord, help me to manage my time well. Open up doors of opportunity where You can use me. Give me discernment to know if there are activities in my life that need to be eliminated so I can take hold of Your purposes for my life. Help me to grow in my ability to use all that You have given me for Your glory. Amen.

Key Area Work List

Week Beginning: _____

1. Connect with God
   A   memory work
   A   prayer
   B   read

2. Grow in community
   A   exercise
   A   small group
   C   play

3. Serve in community
   A   mentor
   C   Matthew party
   A   Prep to preach

4. Family
   A   Time with Deb
   B   Time with kids
   B   Call mom

5. Work
   A   mentor
   C   Matthew party
   A   Prep to preach

6. Domestic
   B   Home projects
   B   Help clean
   B   Car care

7. Physical health
   B   Help cook
   A   Dr.'s appointments
   A   exercise

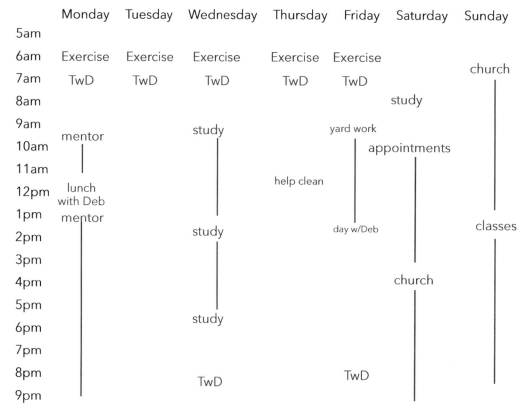

	Monday	Tuesday	Wednesday	Thursday	Friday	Saturday	Sunday
5am							
6am	Exercise	Exercise	Exercise	Exercise	Exercise		church
7am	TwD	TwD	TwD	TwD	TwD		
8am						study	
9am			study		yard work		
10am	mentor					appointments	
11am							
12pm	lunch with Deb			help clean			
1pm	mentor						classes
2pm			study		day w/Deb		
3pm							
4pm						church	
5pm							
6pm			study				
7pm							
8pm					TwD		
9pm			TwD				

Key Area Work List

Week Beginning: _____

1. _____   2. _____
   ___ _____   ___ _____
   ___ _____   ___ _____
   ___ _____   ___ _____

3. _____   4. _____
   ___ _____   ___ _____
   ___ _____   ___ _____
   ___ _____   ___ _____

5. _____   6. _____
   ___ _____   ___ _____
   ___ _____   ___ _____
   ___ _____   ___ _____

7. _____
   ___ _____
   ___ _____
   ___ _____

	Monday	Tuesday	Wednesday	Thursday	Friday	Saturday	Sunday
5am							
6am							
7am							
8am							
9am							
10am							
11am							
12pm							
1pm							
2pm							
3pm							
4pm							
5pm							
6pm							
7pm							
8pm							
9pm							

Standards For Healthy Discipleship

Managing Your Mouth

Jesus said: *"The good man brings good things out of the good stored up in his heart. The evil man brings evil things out of the evil stored up in his heart. For out of the overflow of his heart, his mouth speaks."* (Luke 6:45)

Two things stand out from Jesus in this passage. First, our mouth is connected to our heart; and second, our words reveal what is inside. If we can effectively monitor our mouth, we can discern the temperature of our heart. If cold, insensitive things roll off our lips, you can be sure that our passion to live as Christ is also growing cold. Ephesians 4:29 says: *"Do not let any unwholesome talk come out of your mouths, but only what is helpful for building others up according to their needs, that it may benefit those who listen."*

Today we will evaluate what we say and how we say it. Before we examine several areas of potential danger, take a quick survey to see if this is an area of strength or weakness for you.

1 = No or Never   3 = Sometimes   5 = Yes or Frequently

1. I complain about others.   1 2 3 4 5

2. I have complimented someone today.   1 2 3 4 5

3. I have recently participated in gossip   1 2 3 4 5
(spoken negatively about others).

4. I look for ways to encourage others with my words.   1 2 3 4 5

5. I exaggerate when telling a story.   1 2 3 4 5

6. I have expressed gratitude to someone today.   1 2 3 4 5

7. I have been told I talk too much.   1 2 3 4 5

8. I have excused myself from a   1 2 3 4 5
conversation of gossip.

9. I rationalize why I'm not completely honest.   1 2 3 4 5

10. I have expressed thankfulness to God today.   1 2 3 4 5

11. I speak my assumptions before   1 2 3 4 5
 checking the facts.

12. I think about the impact of my words   1 2 3 4 5
 before speaking.

Now, add up your score for the even numbered statements and record it below, and then add up your score for the odd numbered statements.

> Even Number Score _____   Odd Number Score _____
> From 21-30 This is an area of strength From 6-13
> From 14-20 This needs improvement From 14-20
> From 6-13   Improvement is critical   From 21-30

For a little deeper reflection/self-examination, have someone you know well take the survey on your behalf and ask them to be unreservedly honest (You can find a second copy of the survey in the Appendix, pg. xii).

Managing our mouth and what we say is not easy, but worth the effort because it shows at what depth we are submitting ourselves to Christ and His indwelling Spirit.

From your score on the above survey:
What is an area of strength?
What is an area of weakness?

Describe a time you were complimented or encouraged by someone's words and its affect on you.

Describe a time you were insulted or torn down by someone's words and its affect on you.

Christian Community should be a place where we are built up. As we meet people where they are and love them to where Christ wants them to be, our words will be essential tools for our success. Our trust and confidence within community is directly connected to our communication. There are four major areas where Scripture specifies how we must learn to manage what we say:

(1) Expressing gratitude instead of grumbling
(2) Building others up (encouraging) instead of tearing them down
(3) Confidentiality instead of gossip
(4) Speaking the truth in love instead of being deceptive

Read through the following passages and write 1, 2, 3, or 4, next to the text to match it up with one of the 4 categories above.

_____ *"A man of perverse heart does not prosper; he whose tongue is deceitful falls into trouble."* Proverbs 17:20

_____ *"When words are many, sin is not absent, but he who holds his tongue is wise."* Proverbs 10:19

_____ *"A gossip betrays a confidence, but a trustworthy man keeps a secret."* Proverbs 11:13

_____ *"Reckless words pierce like a sword, but the tongue of the wise brings healing."* Proverbs 12:18

_____ *"Pleasant words are a honeycomb, sweet to the soul and healing to the bones."* Proverbs 16:24

_____ *"He who covers over an offense promotes love, but whoever repeats the matter separates close friends."* Proverbs 17:9

_____ *"He who answers before listening – that is his folly and his shame."* Proverbs 18:13

_____ *". . . the LORD . . . has heard your grumbling . . . Who are we? You are not grumbling against us, but against the LORD.'"* Exodus 16:8

_____ *"Instead, speaking the truth in love, we will grow to become in every respect the mature body of him who is the head, that is, Christ."* Ephesians 4:15

_____ *"Be joyful always; pray continually; give thanks in all circumstances, for this is God's will for you in Christ Jesus."* 1 Thessalonians 5:16-18

_____ *"Without wood a fire goes out; without gossip a quarrel dies down."* Proverbs 26:20

_____ *"Do not let any unwholesome talk come out of your mouths, but only what is helpful for building others up according to their needs, that it may benefit those who listen."* Ephesians 4:29

An old Indian proverb says: "To speak without thinking is to shoot without aiming." Today we highlight the power of our words, and our responsibility to use our words to hit the target of His glory. From now on, establish five healthy ground rules for managing your mouth:

1. Whatever you're told in confidence, do not repeat.

2. Whenever you're tempted to deceive, do not yield.

3. Whenever you're discussing people, do not gossip.

4. Whenever you're prone to disagree, do not slander.

5. Whenever you're tempted to grumble, choose to be grateful.

Prayer Focus:
Based on today's topic and Scriptures, write your own "prayer focus." Take some inspiration from King David's prayer in Psalm 19:14, and then write your own prayer.

Standards For Healthy Discipleship

Creating Effective Accountability & Building Better Boundaries

As a church, we are committed to develop and refine a community of faith where all those who enter into service are provided support, encouragement and accountability.

This devotional is your invitation to commit to this noble calling. As we continue to look over the "Standards for Healthy Discipleship," please realize that these standards are not points of legalism, but boundaries for effective ministry and life.

A boundary is a person's ability to let good things in and keep bad things out. Boundaries are not about keeping rules, but embracing principles. There is a big difference. I choose not to smoke – not because there is a rule which forbids smoking, but because I believe in a principle that says my body is God's temple and I want to take care of it.

People who lack boundaries are regularly compromising their ability to live out what they might "say" are their values. They find themselves either overly committed (living out of balance) or unable to commit (irresponsible living). Fear and anxiety weigh on their ability to say "yes" or "no," and they are inordinately concerned with how they "think" others view them.

As you seek to understand, create and refine better boundaries, it is natural to feel challenged and feel occasional failure, especially as you open yourself up to accountability. If you have been around me for any time, then you've probably heard me say, "We'll never become who we need to be by remaining what we are."

Within community, we begin to expand our objectivity and discover how to embrace healthier boundaries. Accountability forms an increased resolve to live differently; and by living differently, we boost our efforts to change.

We need a combination of three things to make accountability an effective ally. I have been walking with other believers and seeking to have accountable relationships for 40 years. In all that time I have never heard anyone describe how to make accountability successful. We know that we need it, but we are often reluctant to truly embrace it. Much of our resistance to accountability is because we fear that it will threaten our independence and exploit our failures. This is exactly why we also fear the being vulnerable and open, someone might step in and think they need to hold us accountable.

Think of accountability as a triangle. The three pillars that make the accountability triangle are: 1) leadership that drives it, 2) vision that inspires it, and 3) a structure that can sustain it.

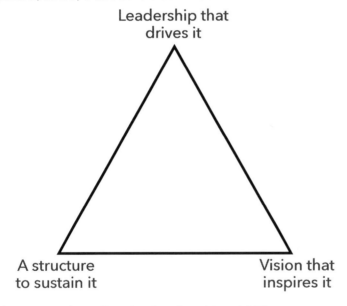

At the top you have "Leadership that drives it". That means someone has to be assertive enough to say, "This is where I, or you, or we, need to be held accountable. This could be a parent, boss, small group leader, mentor or an accountability partner.

The second pillar (to the lower right) is "Vision that inspires it". I must be motivated to submit to accountability. If I cannot see (that's the vision part) why this will be a benefit to me, I'll probably opt out. Kids can smell when this is missing. They will appropriately and intuitively ask: WHY? Why should I do that? Why do I have to do that? Why would I want to do that? If you cannot answer the why, you won't be able to engage people into effective accountability.

The third pillar is "A structure to sustain it." For accountability to happen, there must be some kind of meeting structure where the participants gather regularly and the question pertaining to the need for accountability is asked. This could be a staff meeting, a family pow-wow, a text or phone call. But unless there is an agreed upon structure (time designated to check in and ask the needed questions), accountability will fail.

The last piece to create sustainable accountability is trust. Write the word trust in the middle of the triangle.

In order to foster a culture of growing disciples, there must be a climate of radical acceptance where we can be honest about who we are as well as who we have been. Peter Scazzero, author of *Emotionally Healthy Spirituality,* says: "A church committed to emotional health is a messy place. Skeletons come out of the closet, and we face problems and tensions honestly and directly rather than ignoring them, hoping, or pretending they will somehow go away."

That means we have to nurture the kind of acceptance where our ego can die. I don't need to be right all the time. I don't have to be perfect and fear failure. I can take risks, be honest, make mistakes, and accept responsibility for what I have done, knowing that I am accepted as a child of God, in the process of becoming more like Christ. Sometimes that occurs one victory at a time; and on other occasions, one failure at a time.

Henry Cloud, author of *How People Grow*, reminds us that: "Grace may be available to us but we might not be available to grace. We can be around a lot of acceptance and grace, but until the hurt and guilty places of our hearts are exposed, we do not experience grace, and the gap between our head and our heart continues."

What has been your experience with accountability? Write in the space below whether it was good or bad, effective or not. Did it help you, and did your accountability partners do it in a way that was effective?

What makes the most sense to you about how I have described accountability?

Who could you invite into an accountable relationship? If you have someone or a group of people in mind, do you think you can apply the three pillars into these relationships in order to build better and more effective accountability?

Take a few minutes to think about each of the following areas/issues and see if you can fill in the Vision piece. Write out what the benefit would be for the person if they were successful with each of the below areas.

Sexual purity
Leader – you or a mentor
Vision –
Structure – at your weekly small group

Financial-debt reduction
Leader – your spouse, mentor, small group leader…
Vision –
Structure – over breakfast or after dinner once a week.

Daily time of Solitude with God
Leader – you or a mentor
Vision –
Structure – your weekly accountability meeting or small group or a daily text message.

Bill Hull, in his book, *The Disciple Making Pastor,* says, "To believe you can make true disciples or develop maturity in the lives of others without some form of accountability, is like believing you can raise children without discipline, run a company without rules or lead an army without authority. Accountability is to the Great Commision, what tracks are to a train."

Relational Boundaries

Spiritual success is not arriving at a place where we don't fail. Rather, it's learning from our failures and undergoing refinement by the ongoing reminder that we need grace, love and forgiveness from God as well as from other believers.

When we are unaware of our needs and desires and how to manage them in a healthy way, we are tempted, often unconsciously, to seek out inappropriate relationships to meet those needs, or temporarily satisfy those desires. Building strong self-awareness, healthy boundaries, and trusted relationships (where accountability can happen) are all part of how we avoid crossing lines that violate our values, others and our personal purity. Learning to do this takes time and happens best in an environment where we are doing life with people that we trust, where we can admit our failures and cultivate healthy accountability.

Because we live in a culture that blurs the lines between what is healthy and unhealthy, sexually and relationally, we have written the following relational boundaries. In their absence we unwittingly entangle ourselves in relationships that can become emotionally or sexually inappropriate and thereby threaten our growth and stability. Read through the following seven standards and answer the questions below.

1. I will avoid ongoing one-on-one care for the opposite sex by referring such a person to a more appropriate caregiver.

2. I will refer and encourage man-to-man and woman-to-woman care and support among our church body. I will not be involved in inappropriate physical contact, discuss sexual problems or my marriage problems with any person of the opposite sex, or that I am attracted to in a sexual way.

3. I will make other team/group members my protective allies for relationship accountability.

4. I will pray for the integrity of other team/group members.

5. I will be honest about my life and actions with appropriate team/group members.

6. I will be open for dialogue concerning any possible discrepancies in my moral integrity.

7. I will seek to live out my sexuality in a manner that is consistent with Scripture and honors God through either a healthy heterosexual commitment in marriage or abstinence and celibacy.

What do you think is at the heart of these guidelines?

Have you ever found yourself in a situation where you crossed a line or felt vulnerable to crossing a line and had no one to confide in or receive healthy accountability? How did that feel and where did it take you spiritually?

How would healthy accountability and the above boundaries helped?

Do you have any questions as to the appropriateness of these guidelines? If yes, make some time to process your questions with your ministry leader, a mentor, or a staff member.

Prayer Focus:
"Lord, help me to embrace accountabily, and fear what can happen without accountability. Make me the kind of person who is growing in my ability and insight to set healthier boundaries. Help me to accept others radically and challenge them passionately to live with a greater love for you and others. Help me to build the kind of trust in my relationships that welcomes and models vulnerability and accountability to others. Amen."

Week In Review Questions

1. Share the first draft of your story with your small group or mentor and get some feedback on how it can be refined. If you are reviewing this material with a small group you may want to take a few weeks practicing the telling of both the God story and your story, before moving on.

2. Someone has said that churches don't have money problems, they have stewardship problems. What do you think that means, and what has been your experience in learning to be a more generous person?

3. Describe how you manage your time and what you want to apply from day 33's material to better manage your time.

4. What were your results with our Managing Your Mouth Survey? Where are you the weakest? How did this study impact you?

5. Recall the accountability triangle? Draw it here to reinforce each piece. Where would you like more and better accountability?

Week 8

This is our last week and it is an important conclusion to our Disciples Devotional. We have learned that being a disciple is being a learner. This week we will learn what disciples do when relationships are at their worst; when feelings get hurt and our pride is injured. We will also construct a plan on how we will move forward now that we have more tools for our spiritual journey. I am so thankful that you have made it this to this point. Keep connecting, keep growing and keep serving. It is so worth it!
Love, Pastor Jeff

Consecrating Your Conflict

"Consecration" is not a term we use often and, dare I say, never in conjunction with the word "conflict." But precisely because these terms are somewhat antithetical, I've put them together for today's subject title.

The word "consecration" was used frequently in the Old Testament to refer to people, places, or things that were set aside for God's use. The word means to associate with what is sacred (Ex 13:2, 19:10, 29:37 and 44). "Conflict," on the other hand, has more of a connotation of breaking apart. And we do not usually associate it with anything sacred. What if we could change the way we deal with conflict so instead of making us weaker relationally, it makes us stronger? One of the clearest passages in the New Testament expressing the concept of consecration is 1 Corinthians 6:19-20: *"Do you not know that your body is the temple of the Holy Spirit, who is in you, whom you have received from God? You are not your own, you were bought for a price. Therefore honor God with your body."*

Another passage that calls us to consecrate our relationships is Colossians 3:12-13: *"Therefore, as God's chosen people, holy (consecrated) and dearly loved, clothe yourselves with kindness, humility, gentleness and patience. Bear with each other and forgive whatever grievances you may have against one another..."*

Do you see the word "conflict" in this passage? No, but if you look carefully, you will see how we are to deal with one another due to our sacredness – our being a part of His chosen, Holy people.

That is our focus today – consecrating our conflict. Making sure that we make sacred our relationships with one another in the most difficult of circumstances, when we have hurt one another. Believe me, it's not "if," it's when.

Authors Jeanne Segal and Melinda Smith define conflict as that which arises from differences, both large and small. It occurs whenever people disagree over their values, motivations, perceptions, ideas, or desires. Sometimes these differences appear trivial, but when a conflict triggers strong feelings, a deep personal need is often at the core of the problem. These needs can be a need to feel safe and secure, a need to feel respected and valued, or a need for greater closeness and intimacy.

Because of the underlying need beneath the conflict, resolving conflict is often the price that we pay for deeper levels of intimacy. You don't really know how much someone loves you until you have offended or hurt him or her deeply. Some of us have an acute aversion to conflict; others are gifted at instigating it, few are naturally adept at resolving it. That's why we must address this topic head on. Unaddressed conflict turns into a land mine in the terrain of relationships. If it is not faced, it will remain a barrier to your growth and development as a disciple and who we are as the body of Christ.

As disciples of Christ, we must learn how Jesus wants us to handle our relational hurts and disappointments. Knowing this would take place, Jesus gives us the following instructions:

"If a fellow believer hurts you, go and tell him – work it out between the two of you. If he listens, you've made a friend. If he won't listen, take one or two others along so that the presence of witnesses will keep things honest, and try again. If he still won't listen, tell the church. If he won't listen to the church, you'll have to start over from scratch; confront him with the need for repentance and offer again God's forgiving love" Matthew 18:15-18 (MSG)

As you complete this last week of material, I thank you for working through these important discipleship principles. Ephesians 4:3 says: *"Make every effort to keep this unity of the spirit through the bond of peace."* Relationships falter and the bond of peace is broken when we fail to "make every effort to keep the unity of the spirit." Romans 12:18 says: *"If it is possible, as far as it depends on you, live at peace with everyone."*

The next two day's work will focus on the reality of interpersonal conflict and relational challenges. When we follow God's standards, we learn to practice the presence of God when we need it the most – when we experience our own or someone else's shortcomings. Take a look at the following contrast of healthy and unhealthy ways of addressing conflict.

Unhealthy
An inabilty to respond appropriately to the needs and concerns of others.

Healthy
An ability to respond appropriately to the needs and concerns of others.

Unhealthy
Explosive, defensive, hurtful, angry or passive aggressive reactions to others.

Healthy
Calm, non-defensive, patient, compassionte, and respectful responses to others.

Unhealthy
Punitive reactions that seek to inflict hurt, shame, guilt, withdrawal of love and rejection.

Healthy
Patient responses that seek to move towards understanding, clarity, win-win solutions, healthy boundaries and forgiveness.

Unhealthy
A propensity to avoid, isolate, gossip and abandon relationships.

Healthy
A belief and commitment to face and address issues, hurt and misunderstanding with gentleness and respect.

Look over the above contrast between healthy and unhealthy conflict, write a few sentences about where you need to grow and become more healthy and why.

To consecrate our conflict, to make it healthy, we need both a commitment and a process. In accordance with God's Word, we hope to equip our church family (members) to develop a deepening conviction about how to handle any conflicts that arise as we connect, grow and serve together. We, therefore, ask you to make the following commitment.

My COMMITMENT:

– In all conflicts, I will seek to act in a Christ-like manner and not give into my natural (flesh) human feelings and emotions.

– I will grow in my emotional self-awareness (being conscious of my moment-to-moment emotional experience) and the ability to manage my feelings appropriately. This is a skill that can be developed when we are committed to truly being a part of a loving community.
Emotional awareness helps you:
- Understand what is really troubling other people
- Understand yourself, including what is really troubling you
- Stay motivated until the conflict is resolved
- Communicate clearly and effectively
- Attract and influence others through healthy, loving choices

– I will pray and seek the Lord's comfort and guidance in the matter. I will not share an offense with another person, unless it is a single (as in one) mentor who can help me approach the matter with accountability, maturity and expediency.

– I will not seek to find others who have been offended, nor will I seek to validate my hurt by finding other potential mediators before meeting with the person who has offended me.

– If I hear another person being criticized, I will exhort the individual criticizing either to go to the party in question and deal with it directly, or refrain from speaking against them. I will encourage them to deal with the issue so it won't interfere with the unity of the body.

Prayer Focus:
Take a few minutes today and ask the Lord if there is anyone in your life with whom you have unresolved conflict. If so, take a moment to allow the Lord to speak to you about that relationship. Try to not rush away from this place of stillness but to allow Him to speak to you clearly. If any awareness of any unresolved issue rises, simply tell the Lord that you need His strength to do the right thing.

Consecrating Your Conflict

Today as we continue to see how Jesus calls us to honor one another and Him in the wake of conflict and hurt, we will look at the actual instructions that He gave to address issues in a way that creates healing and not more hurt, alienation or confusion.

The PROCESS to follow (as defined in Matthew 18:15-20):

– First, I will go to the person alone who has offended me and seek to resolve our differences and restore the relationship. I will value the restoration of the relationship rather than expose that person's possible sin. I will listen to his/her point of view and seek to understand his/her perspective on the issue.

– If going to the person first does not resolve the conflict, I will seek the help of a third party to help both of us determine what we need to do to honor God in our relationship. I will make sure that this third party is a neutal spiritually mature person with regard to this issue. I will keep an open mind to the advice of the third party and seek to change my attitude and actions as I am advised.

– If the third party cannot effect a resolution, and agrees with my concern, I will seek the help of two or three other witnesses who can intercede in the matter and seek to honor God in this conflict. (See step-by-step process for conflict resolution in Appendix, page vi).

As a last resort, if the conflict cannot be resolved through the support of church leadership, I will act in a manner pleasing to God, even if it means distancing myself from the source of the conflict, while also trying to extend an openness for reconciliation.

Have you ever had someone confront some aspect of your walk? If so, what went well, and what didn't?

What do you think keeps people from following the Biblical process for conflict resolution?

Do you feel equipped to follow the Biblical process? If not, what would keep you from pursuing it?

In order to create better boundaries in our church family, we have added the following principles to help us to proactively prepare ourselves to help one another recover from a time of rebellion, or distraction that could pull any one of us off course. Both Matthew 24:10 and 1 Timothy 4:1-5, tell us that many will fall away. In Mark 4, Jesus was very clear that some seed (the Word) would fall on weed-infested ground (cares and worries of this life), choking out God's truth. Fortunately, God's Word also tells us how we can reach out to one another to help confront the things that choke out our spiritual life. Read through the following principles and standards and make any comments that you would like to process during your "Week in Review" meeting.

1. Time to Change
The Matthew 18 passage suggests that the progression in efforts to reconcile a broken relationship comes over a period of time. Any struggling party needs time to process each discussion, and make the needed changes.

"… be patient with each person, attentive to individual needs."
(1 Th 5:14 [MSG])

How important is it to give people time to grow and change while struggling with some personal issue or conflict?

2. Levels of Ministry

We have sought to rate each of our ministry/service positions in a manner consistent with the level of spiritual maturity needed to participate.

– Level 1: A "seeker" level, where those who are still searching can find a place to participate and serve at an entry level.

– Level 2: A "new believer" level, where those who are newly converted might find a higher level of spiritual participation compatible with the new beginning.

– Level 3: An "adolescent" believer, who is showing clear growth and needs to be given more and greater responsibility to develop their walk and service.

– Level 4: A "mature" believer, who has shown faithfulness and displayed Christ-like attitudes in a variety of experiences. They are equipped or ready for any task that fits their gift mix.

Can you see in your own life how you have passed through, or are still in, one of these levels of spiritual growth?

What have you learned by doing *A Disciple's Devotional* that will help you to grow in your own spiritual development?

3. Humility and Restoration

"Brothers, if someone is caught in a sin, you who are spiritual should restore him gently. But watch yourself, or you also may be tempted. Carry each other's burdens, and in this way you will fulfill the law of Christ." Galatians 6:1-2

Paul helps us see that our attitude should always be humble and our approach gentle. The goal for any admonishment should be reconciliation, which must include a willingness to provide support (carry one another's burdens) for the party in question.

How would you want someone to "confront" you if you were involved in some area of sin that was doing you and/or your family and others harm?

4. Confidentiality Confusion

When an individual endangers oneself or others, the issue needs to be brought to the most appropriate person or persons for greater protection for those involved. If someone is bringing others into a clear compromise of values (sexual or physical abuse, for example), the subject or person in question needs to be addressed in a clear and healthy way.

If someone asked you to keep something confidential that endangered someone else, what would you do?

5. Restoration Guidelines

If a believer is struggling or fallen, he or she may be asked to step back from one or more levels of service (described under #2.) until the problem area has been resolved. We will pursue restoration with all parties as they are willing. Regardless of their responsiveness or lack thereof, we will seek to maintain support, encouragement and accountability.

Do you think asking someone to step back for a period of time is a good idea or a bad idea and why?

Following the principles outlined in Matthew 18 and Galatians 6, a leader who has fallen away could be asked to step back from ministry involvement. Because each person and situation is unique, the leadership team overseeing the given individual will provide a restoration plan for support and direction for the emotional, spiritual and relational needs of the leader involved. Because we are commanded in Scripture to submit to those in leadership, restoration to ministry involvement can only be accomplished through cooperative relationships.

What do you see as helpful in this process?

What do you think might be difficult about this process?

Today we have focused on one of those challenging realities that, if ignored, will blindsided us; but, if prepared, we can actually utilize conflict, or the knowledge of someone struggling, as a way to extend God's grace and kindness.

At which level of ministry do you see yourself?

What would equip you to be able to help a fallen friend to move toward restoration?

Prayer Focus:
As you go to prayer today, let's intercede together for a growing number of YC disciples who will embrace our mission and vision, and commit to live the life. Maybe you know of a fallen brother or sister in Christ who needs support – take a minute or two and ask God to draw them back to Himself. Ask if there is anything He wants you to do reach out in love to help him or her move forward.

The Power of Alignment

Increase your Effectiveness

As we close out our 40 days together we want to maximize what we have learned and move forward together to be the people God has called us to be. To do this we will now try to bring all of what we have focused on into action. This can be accomplished as we embrace a powerful principle called the POWER OF ALIGNMENT.

Ephesians 4:4-6:
"There is one body and one Spirit – just as you were called to one hope when you were called – one Lord, one faith, one baptism; one God and Father of all, who is over all and through all and in all."

This section of Ephesians starts off with the declaration of our oneness: "ONE BODY." The author, Paul, then goes on to give a very clear expression of what I refer to as alignment (oneness) – *"...one Lord, one faith, one baptism, one God, and one Father of all, who is over all and in all."* When we are on the same page we have an increased opportunity for success. Paul tells us we must have a degree of solidarity, a set of fundamental principles to fulfill our spiritual mission. Most of chapter 4 in Ephesians revolves around the work of this "ONE BODY."

The person trying to live a spiritual life apart from the Biblical concept of church (Body of Christ) will be frustrated and spiritually sluggish. It would be like riding a bike with flat tires. I mean you could do it, but why would you?

On the other hand, alignment within the body creates an increased level of effectiveness. I can be a church attendee (involved in groups and activities), but if I do not understand my purpose for being there and the difference the Lord wants to make through me, I might be going against the flow.

I just had front-end alignment service on my car. Prior to having the alignment, I literally had to muscle the steering wheel to keep the car traveling straight – a constant fight! When parents can't agree on a parenting style, their kids know it. They do what any red-blooded child would do – they work one parent against the other. If mom disapproves, they go to dad and vice-versa. That's a marriage out of alignment.

It is true for any business, any marriage, and especially any church. When we are on the same page and have the same set of goals and commitments, we will be amazed at what God will do.

This was exactly what James, the brother of Jesus, was driving at when he said: *"… faith by itself, if it is not accompanied by action, is dead"* (Ja 2:17). For many believers, their faith lacks luster because it lacks intentionality. Their spiritual wheels are spinning and they feel the frustration of being stuck in their growth. A Godly goal puts rubber to the road. It gives traction to the spiritual concepts that propel our growth.

The problem with many church-goers is that they can be fooled into thinking they have done their spiritual duty for the week. Attending church is a great goal. But if I walk away with no clearer perspective of specific things I am called to do day by day, I have only played a religious game. I have had motion without movement.

What would you say to a person who claims they want (have a goal) to be more loving but are consistently impatient, rude, and often angry? Or a person who says they want to be debt-free but continues to max out their credit cards and fails to keep track of what they spend on a daily basis? Or someone claiming to want to lose 30 pounds but continue to eat fast food, a bag of chips a day and tasty sweets. Oh yea, they also say the reason they don't work out is because the local gym is just a meat market. I think in every case we would say there's a problem with the person's strategy; their ability to do what it takes to become the person they want to be simply isn't working. When this happens, it doesn't matter how much they "want to" do anything. Until their "want to" becomes a "will do," it's just not going to happen. What I see over and over in the men and women who consistently practice the disciplines is their "want to" gets turned into a "can do."

Have you ever set out to achieve a wonderful goal but didn't have alignment from other parties that were critical for your goal to happen? For example, being debt-free as a family but your spouse just refuses to curtail spending. Write an example or two where you have seen alignment sabotaged. What went wrong and what was needed for better alignment?
Your examples:

Now shift and write about a couple of occasions where you have seen alignment work for the sake of a mutual goal.

What do you think the following passage has to do with alignment? List out what kinds of attitudes and behaviors are critical for healthy alignment.

Ephesians 4:1-6 &11-16

How important do you think it is for our church to have alignment? How would our efforts toward mentoring be more powerful if everyone embraced mentoring as a goal? What other ways do you think we could encourage and train every YCer to learn to share their faith and the big God Story with others?

What stands out to you the most from today's topic and Scriptures?

Prayer Focus:
Close your time today thanking God for whatever degree of alignment you have enjoyed with others and ask Him to help you to make the appropriate changes, to be better aligned with Christ, His church and mission.

The Power of Alignment

As our staff and Council (elders) deliberated over things that would bring us stronger alignment to God's purposes, we identified one clear achievable objective that every YCer, indeed every child of God, would be able to achieve. Rick Warren, author of *The Purpose Driven Life*, says: "Nothing becomes dynamic until it becomes specific." You cannot illustrate that you are loving if there are no specific loving behaviors that flow from your life. I can proclaim that I love my wife but if there are no specific actions coupled with my proclamation, she will remain unconvinced.

Our strategy of Connect, Grow and Serve (and the core disciplines that go with them) coupled with our Vision are the means to the end. They are the tools that assist us to become the people God has called us to be (Christ-like), and fulfill the mission He has given us. There are several Biblical terms that describe our ultimate goal and some of the characteristics that should indicate that we are well on our way. *Mature* (He 12:12; Ep 4:15-16), *godly* (1 Ti 4:7-9), *Christ-like* (2 Co 3:18; Ep 4:24 & 5:1&2), *the fruit of the Spirit* (Ga 5:22-23), the love that should be the dominant characteristic of our lives (1 Co 13), and the *ability to share the Gospel and disciple/mentor others* toward spiritual maturity (He 5:12-14). If these traits and characteristics are not evident, there is a serious issue with how we practice our Christianity.

As we all seek to be more loving, better disciples, mentors and missionaries, we should take aim at those things and articulate how we are going to align ourselves to Christ's calling. Each of these is exactly what God has revealed as His plan. When we do so, we are simply embracing God's agenda as our own our strategy and vision.

Dallas Willard says: "You may find that your commitment is remarkably flabby and thin because it has never been translated into how you spend your time. Now is the time for decision and especially for planning. God changes lives in response to faith. But just as there is no faith that does not act, so there is no act without some plan. Faith grows from the experience of acting on plans and discovering God to be acting with us....This will come down to what you do on Sunday, Monday, Tuesday, Wednesday, Thursday, Friday and Saturday."

This is the task of alignment – pointing our lives, time, and activities in God's direction. Look over each piece of our strategy (Connect, Grow & Serve) and the four "I am" statements and then set a specific goal to move in that direction. I have given several examples of a goal for each area. You can choose one of these or you might have another. Remember that a Good Goal is S.M.A.R.T.

Specific
Measurable
Attainable
Relevant
Time-bound

When we all set smart goals in the same areas the principle of alignment creates exponential results. If you remember the "I am a disciple" statement you'll recall that the "connect, grow serve" strategy is woven into that commitment. The following "Discipleship Plan" was created to help each of us stay focused on the habits and disciplines that we need to most effectively grow spiritually. Each area has a set of disciplines that we call "Core disciplines." You can select any combination to build into your personal discipleship plan. You might want to consult a mentor if it doesn't seem clear as to what combination would be the most helpful for you. This is where the rubber meets the road. *A Disciple's Devotional* culminates into this plan.

Over the weeks we have looked at what disciples are, how disciples grow, what the disciplines are, and how they reinforce and develop a consistent walk with Christ and His Spirit.

As you look at the "My Spiritual Growth Plan," here are a few things to consider. Be sure to use the SMART method for clarity. Here are some general guidelines.

1. For "Connect daily with God through prayer and Bible engagement" be sure to have a specific place, time, and set of disciplines that you can follow through on daily. To support this goal, identify an accountability partner for follow through.

2. For "Grow with others in community" be sure to have a specific group of individuals with whom you gather. This could be a small group, a ministry team, a mentor or a combination of all three. Think of a way you can pursue the idea of "doing life together." This is accomplished when you tie more than one week community, and make it a point to practice spiritual disciplines with those individuals when you are together. Our Garage Gyms (see a description of a Garage Gym in the appendix) are examples of one way to create a stronger community for spiritual growth, and build a stronger accountability for important spiritual choices. This kind of increased togetherness can have a huge impact on an individual's growth.

3. For "Serve with others in community". I suggest thinking through the following expressions of service. Here is where alignment comes into play.

- Do you know your spiritual gifts? If not, our SHAPE class is a great next step goal.

- Have you taken the Mentoring Experience and are you using a clear plan to mentor someone spiritually? If not, the Mentoring Experience will give you the skills to build your personal confidence.

- Are you confident sharing your faith and the Big God story with others? If you would like more experience with both, our Missionary Experience class will propel you forward.

- If you are not serving in a scheduled way (serving with some team on a weekly basis), find a YC team, or contact one of the parachurch groups in our community (a list of these are provided in the appendix).

- Give financially to the ministry of your church. Being a faithful giver is a mark of spiritual maturity. When we give faithfully we live out our commitment to God's mission in and through our financial stewardship. Consider using our online giving app as a way to both honor God through faithfulness and being a blessing to the work of our church's ministry.

4. The only additional goal that we encourage you to add into your spiritual growth plan is to think through what you are intentionally doing to develop your self awareness, especially as it ties back into your ability to grow in love. This too is tied to the spiritual disciplines. This goal is at the heart of your spiritual growth because it is the ultimate test of everything else (1 Co 13).

MY SPIRITUAL GROWTH PLAN

C.S. Lewis: "Put first things first and second things are thrown in. Put second things first and lose both first and second things."

Out of my commitment and love for Christ, I will seek to build a strong and intimate connection to God, His word, His people, and His purposes through the following goals. Review our Spiritual Disciplines on page 114 to help you fill out your Spiritual Growth Plan.

1. **Connecting** daily through prayer and Bible engagement

My goal is to be more like Christ by practicing habits (disciplines) of prayer and Bible engagement through the disciplines of (circle your answers)

Prayer:
-Gratitude
-Fasting
-Petition
-Solitude/Silence
-Examination/Elimination
-Sabbath

Bible Engagement:
-Meditation
-Memorization
-Study
-Worship

Place:
Time:
Accountability Partner(s):

2. **Grow** in community through faithful participation in a small group

My goal is to gather regularly with: _____

Where:
When:
Our Disciplines: Together we will practice (circle your answers)...
-Accountability
-Sharing Resources
-Encouragement
-Intercession
-Worship
-Fellowship
-Hospitality
-Cooperate Gratitude
-Confession

3. Serve in community through...
(this area will have several sub-goals , choose only those that apply to you).
The Experience class schedule* for the following season/year can be found online at yosemitechurch.com/connect/yc-workshops or on the Yosemite Church app.

To be equipped to serve:
-Learning how God has SHAPED me by taking the Shape Experience
When:

-Learning to mentor by attending the Mentoring Experience
When:

-Learning to reach out (be a missionary) by taking the Missionary Experience
When:

I will serve by using my giftedness weekly by....
-Mentoring _____using the GROWTH plan.

-Reaching out to _____to share my faith.

-Giving financially to my church by tithing

-Other...

* The Experience Classes apply to those who attend Yosemite Church.

4. Grow in **self awareness** and being loving.

My goal is to grow in my self-awareness and love by:

Potentials goals:
-Memorize 1 Corinthians 13 to distinguish what love really is.

-Learn to set healthier boundaries in a kind and patient manner.

-Read *Emotionally Healthy Spirituality* as a way to become more loving.

-Identify and eliminate a specific distraction in my life that makes me impatient or preoccupied with things that get in the way of my ability to love well. Use the ABC method (described in week 4) to break the patterns of this world that influence my thinking.

Now that you have completed you Spiritual Growth Plan go to Appendix xvii to complete your final version. On the next page is an example of how I filled mine out.

I am filled with excitement and anticipation even as I write these potential goals. There is no question that as we become who God wants us to be, as described in each of the "I am's," we will bear fruit. It is God's will that you become more loving, that you practice spiritual disciplines, that you learn to mentor and disciple others and that you prepare to share your faith with others.

I want to invite you to commit with me, to God, and to our church that you will accept the challenge to complete your own Discipleship Plan (My Plan for Spiritual Growth) and begin to work that plan with at least one other person, while seeking to grow in each of these areas.

Prayer Focus:
"Lord, we can do many things, but unless we are aligned to what You are doing, we could miss our purpose for being here. Help us to find ourselves in You and Your purposes. Amen"

My Spiritual Growth Plan

CONNECT

Prayer & Bible Engagement:

-Praying thru Roms. 12
-Confession
-SOAPing Roms. 8
-Meditation

When/Where:

In my office/study area
and back patio
between 4:30am-6am

Accountability:

Garage Gym

GROW

Who:

-Stretch leaders
-Garage Gym
-Management Team

When:

-Tue. am
-Mon/Wed. am

Where:

-Garage gym
-office

Our Disciplines:

Fellowship
Gratitude
Confession
Die to self
Encouragement
Hospitality

SERVE

To be equipped to serve:
-leading the Experience classes
-reviewing the GROWTH acrostic
-leading the Men's stretch

I will serve by:
-teaching/training more leaders to teach the
experience classes
-modeling the mentoring of others by inteni-
tonally mentoring the stretch/Men's leaders
and at least one adolesent youth
-Mentor Kevin, Bill, Nick

SELF AWARENESS

Potential Goals:

-reviewing regularly the biblical bases for both
-practicing the ABC's of self awareness
-reading one of the following books: <u>Stretngthening the Soul</u> by Ruth Burton
<u>Presence</u> by Benner

Space & Humility

You did it! You went the full 40 days. Congratulations!

The goal of the devotional has been to help you to create the space needed to strengthen your faith; to make your walk with Christ sustainable and rich, so you can more humbly love and serve others as an expression of your love for Him. The spiritual disciplines are inseparable from the life of a growing disciple. Over the last eight weeks you have allowed me to poke you with spiritual tools and topics that are all designed to help you look more deeply at your own resolve to be a disciple of Jesus, a functioning member of the Body of Christ and an ambassador of His Great Commandment and Great Commission (Connect, Grow, and Serve). To obtain greater personal insight of the things that hold you back and a humble pursuit of the habits that can propel you forward.

One of the intended outcomes of the devotional was that, by doing the daily material, you would create or re-engage the spiritual habit of connecting with God daily, and by doing the weekly review questions with others, you would begin or re-engage a habit of growing with others in community. These two overarching habits set the foundation for building a sustainable life of faith and service. This is where we need space for God in times of solitude and space for others within community.

On our journey as disciples our challenge is to acquire the kind of tools that will not only equip us to live out God's presence and purposes, in our own lives, but to also equip others to do so. This was Paul's motivation in 2 Timothy 2:2 (MSG) where he says, *"Throw yourself into this work for Christ. Pass on what you heard from me to reliable leaders who are competent to teach others."*

Growing in our spiritual habits enable us to manage our space; the world that we have been intrusted with. As we do so, we will, like a well watered plant, grow and naturally bear fruit. This is what Jesus was saying in John 15:7: *"If you remain in me and my words remain in you, ask whatever you wish and it will be given to you. This is to my Father's glory that you bear much fruit."* The bearing of "much fruit" requires a perpetual connection.

The growing disciple learns to manage their space; this makes room for God to speak, to be seen, understood, embraced and revealed. When we live lives that lack spiritual discipline; submission and self-control-spiritual focus and awareness – (Ga 5:23-26; 1 Pe 1:13 & 2 Tm 2:7) we find the world around us consuming everything we have and leaving no room, or space, or recovery. Conversely when we learn to walk in the Spirit we learn how to manage and maintain our space; we create room for three perpetual next steps.

1. **Disciples never stop practicing their fundamentals;** Connecting with Jesus daily, Growing with others in community, and Serving out of the overflow of Christ's presence in them. The next step for me, and you, to thrive spiritually, is to keep doing the fundamentals of the cycle of spiritual growth. If these are not rooted in your schedule they will easily get pushed out of your calendar. Those who lose spiritual focus didn't maintain spiritual discipline in the fundamentals. This requires space in your schedule; to be unhurried with God and others.

2. **Disciples never stop learning.** They have a foundation that doesn't change but know that they live in a culture that is constantly changing. Therefore, they seek to be a continual learner; they learn how to apply God's unchanging truth to a world that is desperate for the stability of an unchanging God. They learn to embrace other's perspectives to see how they fit; how they complement truth or if they are antithetical to truth. They learn to be inquisitive, read new books or take classes to develop some aspect of their gifting; they seek to learn more about whoever they are with and give room for the spontaneous. This requires space in your conversations so you don't fill every interaction with just your own voice.

3. **Disciples never stop seeking spiritual discernment** – spiritual awareness. *"Keeping in step with the Spirit"* (Ga 5:26) means that we are always vulnerable to getting out of step. Therefore, this is both being self-aware; so we can continue to die to the things that will relentlessly plague the human race, and God-aware; so we will recognize how Jesus wants us to be stepping into opportunities to extend His love and grace to others and make Him known. This requires space in our heads so we can filter out human noise (the patterns of this world) and hear His voice of truth.

In John 21 Jesus continued to do this with Peter by asking him a simple question that also taught him a crucial lesson. Three times Jesus asks, *"Do you love me?"* Peter, "hurt" that Jesus would ask him three times, says, *"Yes, you know that I love you!"* Jesus said, *"Feed my sheep".* The purposes of God are not just that we would grow more deeply in our love for Him (do you love me) but that we would also be more committed to love those He is sending us to (feeding His sheep). I can always gage whether my love for Jesus is maturing by how my love for others is growing.

When we are connecting well with Jesus in our times of personal solitude we will find a renewable energy to love others and serve humbly. Jesus asking Peter three times if he loved him, seems appropriate in light of Peter's denial; once for each time he denied him. Jesus wasn't trying to hurt Peter, when he asked him three times if he loved him, rather he was helping Peter to increase his ability to walk in humility. It must have been a little humiliating for Peter to face the Lord after such a blatant transgression, especially after his impressive declaration to never do so. Peter did not learn humility the easy way but the hard way. This too is the route that most of us will take. Humility isn't something we stumble into but something we grow into. The ultimate test of how well we understanding and embracing God's agenda for our life is how humbly we can relinquishing ours. At the core of a maturing disciple is the ability, through humility, to relinquish our agenda for His.

My definition of humility ties nicely into our strategy (Connect, Grow, Serve). Humility is the ability to live dependently on God, interdependantly on others with a passion and commitment to serve. It takes breaking free of our compulsion to be independant of God and others to live out our calling.

Describe how you are learning to be more humble in each of the following areas.

1) Your dependence on God.

2) Your interdependence on others.

3) Your passion and commitment to serve.

Prayer Focus:
Thank you for taking this journey with me. My prayers continue to go up for everyone who picks up *A Disciple's Devotional* that it will equip them to takes up their cross to follow Jesus.

Take a few minutes today and join me in prayer for others going through the devotional, for our church family and for your own resolve to follow Jesus with greater focus. Ask the Lord impress on your heart who you can "pass on" what you are learning. Who could you begin to mentor? Write their name here and say a prayer for them that would begin to prepare their heart for a deeper more intentional journey into following Jesus.

Week In Review Questions

1. What did you learn about healthy boundaries from Day 36? Have you struggled to set healthy boundaries with the opposite sex? Are there any adjustments that you need to make to improve your boundaries?

2. Conflict is not easy, but if we can see it as a sacred part of our life, together we can face it with gentleness, compassion and respect. How did this material influence your own perspective on conflict and the help you can offer to those who have fallen?

3. Where in the contrast between healthy and unhealthy conflict did you see where you need to grow?

4. What did you glean from Days 38 & 39's material on Alignment? Do you think you are becoming more aligned with what disciples are called to do, and with who we are as a church? If so, how?

5. Please share a few of your goals from your own "Spiritual Development Plan."

6. Do you think a person can manage the space for their schedule, conversations and thoughts well without discipline, why or not?

7. How does Pastor Jeff's definition of Humility sit with you, does it make sense? How are you growing in your ability to walk in humility (greater dependance on God, interdependence on others and passion to serve)?

8. What is your biggest take-away from doing this devotional? Do you think you could use the devotional as a tool to help someone else grow in their faith? Who could you begin to invest in with great intentionality? Why or why wouldn't you want to begin to mentor someone?

Appendix

Bible References

All references are to the New International Version (NIV), unless otherwise noted, as below:

CEV ...... Contemporary English Version
ESV ...... English Standard Version
GW .... God's Word
KJV ...... King James Version
LB .... The Living Bible
MSG ..... The Message
NLT ...... New Living Translation
Ph ...... J.B. Phillips Translation
TEV ...... Today's English Version

Statement Of Faith

What We Believe – Yosemite Church, Merced CA

In essential beliefs– we have unity.
"There is one Body and one Spirit... there is one Lord, one faith, one baptism, and one God and Father of us all." Ephesians 4:4-6

About God
God is the creator and Ruler of the universe. He has eternally existed in three persons: the Father, the Son and the Holy Spirit. These three are co-equal and are one God. Gn 1:1,26,27; 3:22; Ps 90:2; Mt 28:19; 1 Pt 1:2; 2 Co 13:14

About Mankind
We are all made in the spiritual image of God, to be like Him in character. We are the supreme object of God's creation. Although mankind has tremendous potential for good, we are marred by an attitude of disobedience toward God called "sin". This attitude separates us from God. Gn 1:27; Ps 8:3-6; Is 53:6a; Rm 2:23; Is 59:1-2

About Eternity
We all were created to exist forever. We will either exist eternally separated from God by sin, or in union with God through forgiveness and salvation. The place of eternal separation from God is called Hell. Heaven is the place of eternal union and eternal life with God. Jn 3:16; Rm 6:23; Rv 20:15 (Hell); Mt 25:41; Rv 21:27 (Heaven) 94

About Jesus Christ
Jesus Christ is the Son of God. He is co-equal with the Father. Jesus lived a sinless human life and offered Himself as the perfect sacrifice for the sins of all by dying on a cross. He arose from the dead after three days to demonstrate His power over sin and death. He ascended to Heaven's glory and will return again to earth to reign as King of Kings, and Lord of Lords. Mt 1:22-23; Is 9:6; Jn 1:1-5; Jn 14:10-30; He 4:14-15; 1 Co 15:3-4; Rm 1:3-4; Ac 1:9-11; 1 Tm 6:14,15; Ti 2:13

About Salvation
Salvation is a gift from God to mankind. We can never make up for our sin by self-improvement or good works. Only by trusting in Jesus Christ as God's offer of forgiveness can we be saved from sin's penalty. Eternal life begins the moment we receive Jesus Christ into our life by faith. Rm 5:1; Rm 6:23; Ep 2:8,9; Jn 1:12, 14:6; Ti 3:5; Ga 3:26

About Eternal Security
Because God gives us eternal life through Jesus Christ, the believer is secure in the salvation for eternity. Salvation is maintained by the grace and power of God, not by the self-effort of the Christian. It is the grace and keeping power of God that gives this security.

About The Holy Spirit
The Holy Spirit is equal with the Father and the Son as God. He is present in the world to make mankind aware of our need for Jesus Christ. He also lives in every Christian from the moment of salvation. He provides the Christian with power for living, understanding of spiritual truth, and guidance in doing what is right. The Christian seeks to live under His control daily. 1 Co 2:12, 3:16; 2 Co 3:17; Jn 16:7-13; Jn 14:16, 17; Ac 1:8; Ep 1:13, 5:1; Ga 5:25

About The Bible
The Bible is God's word to all mankind. It was written by human authors, under the supernatural guidance of the Holy Spirit. It is the supreme source of truth for Christian beliefs and living. Because it is inspired by God, it is truth without any mixture of error. 2 Tm 1:13, 3:16; 2 Pt 1:20,21; Ps 119:105, 160, 12:6; Pr 30:5, Jn 10:29; 2 Tm 1:12; He 7:25; 10:10,14; 1 Pt 1:3-5 95

About Marriage
Based on the teaching of the Scriptures in both the Old and New Testaments, that marriage is an institution ordained by God from the foundation of the world, and intended as a lifelong union of one man and one woman. This idea is supported by the account of creation in Gn chapters 1 and 2. Gn 1:26-28 provides that God created man in His own image, both male and female. This passage teaches that a unity of one man and one woman is in some way necessary to fully represent the image of God in mankind. Gn 1:26-28, Gn 2:15-25, Mt 19:4-6, Ep 5:22-32

General Ministry Description

General Description

Seek to understand and live out the healthy standards of discipleship. Commit to uphold our Mission, Vision, and Values for ministry and pursue a lifestyle that reflects the Biblical principles.

General Conduct

Be open to the input of others.
Be on time for meetings.
Be prompt in returning phone calls.
Be a learner, i.e. taking advantage of leadership development opportunities and training.
Be quick to resolve conflict.
Be committed to speak positively about others.
Be committed to the spiritual disciplines of prayer, Bible reading, journaling, church attendance, meditation and memorization, financial giving, fellowship, and reaching out to those far from God.
Be a team player. Serve in an area of ministry that reflects your giftedness and connection to others in service.

Resolving Conflict & Relational Hurt

When Difficult Things Need to be Said
1. Ask for some one-on-one time with the person in question.
2. Speak about your concern directly to the person involved.
3. Check out the situation from the other person's perspective to make sure you've interpreted the details correctly.
4. Listen and confirm any significant details by paraphrasing.
5. Express your perspective. Be clear if any change of behavior is needed. If he or she has articulated the issue well and identified what would be adjusted, you can confirm those observations, but be clear as to how things would look different in the future.
6. Ask if there are any other thoughts or input. Ask him or her to tell you what you are saying, to ensure understanding.
7. Thank him or her for working on this valuable relationship.
8. Ask if you are both OK with each other.
9. Touch base within the next 24 hours to be sure you are both OK.

Tips for Keeping Things on Track
1. Remember to talk using "I" statements, instead of "you" statements.
2. Ask for a time out if emotions become too intense.
3. Slow down the conversation and mutually seek to speak with grace.
4. Seek first to understand the other person's perspective before being understood.
5. Ask if you understand the issue correctly, or if you are missing something.
6. Once you think you have heard the other person, use reflective listening* to be sure you have understood both message and emotions.
*Reflective listening: Such as, "So what I hear you say…", "Let me see if I got this right?"; or rephrase their statement as a question
7. Always end by thanking the person.
8. Remember that you may need more than one meeting to get things resolved.
9. If it appears the situation is not moving toward resolution, ask the party to pick a person to join the discussion.
Breaks are particularly important if one party is emotionally flooded.

Creating A Restoration Plan

The following steps provide an outline for writing/documenting and facilitating a Restoration Plan, and the communication that needs to accompany the process.

Preliminary Steps:
1. Party in question will be asked to step back from one or more levels of leadership, depending on the issue at hand. Be sure all areas of involvement are considered and appropriate leaders are informed via phone or personal contact.

2. A written plan of restoration will need to be crafted by the supervising leader following the steps below:

Outline: To serve as a template in building a specific restoration plan.

1. Identify a support person to walk alongside, pray with, listen to, and care for the individual stepping back from ministry.

2. Select an appropriate resource: curriculum, group, or counselor for the needed emotional and spiritual healing; define the time and commitment necessary for completion.

3. Re-evaluate by support person, ministry lead and staff contact, after a minimum break of 3 months to evaluate if reinstatement is appropriate or more work is needed. This process should include a review of the healthy standards of discipleship.

4. Communicate to the appropriate leadership the gist of the issues and upcoming reinstatement of the individual into leadership.

5. Reinstate the leader with a formal blessing, i.e. leadership group, encouraging and praying with the individual.

Sample Restoration Plan & Behavioral Agreement

Name:_____

As a Pastor of Yosemite Church, I want you to know that I value you and your relationship with Christ. I appreciate that you have been honest about your past and have agreed to respect several boundaries that are very important for Yosemite Church to maintain an environment that communicates God's love and a confidence that children, families, and individuals are important, safe, and respected.

We at YC are all broken-followers of Christ in need of accountability. This Restoration Plan and Behavioral agreement is designed to help you grow in your relationship with Christ while you fulfill your obligations. You have already been asked to step down from any leadership role and responsibility in accordance with our leadership standards; however, you are allowed to serve in your ministries.

Therefore, I am asking you to read this document and agree that you understand the boundaries. Signing this document will indicate that you are willing to adhere to these requirements.

Boundary #1 – Immediately cut all ties of communication with any relationship(s) that was/were inappropriate and promptly report any communication attempt on their behalf with you or your spouse, your pastor and your accountability partner.

This will demonstrate your desire to turn from your mistake and begin repairing correct relationships. This also ensures that you are taking the necessary steps to hold yourself accountable in the sight of God and man.

Our Motivation: To know that you are working to be faithful to God, to grow spiritually and to develop healthy relationships.

Name of Pastor: _____

Name of Accountability Partner: _____

Boundary #2 – Seek professional counseling for your marriage.

Marriage is a sacred union between a man and a woman that is held up as an example of Christ and His church. Seeking help is a powerful demonstration of your love and devotion to this union.

Our Motivation: To know that you are passionate about pursuing a healthy marriage relationship, one that is rooted deeply in a commitment to Christ and one another.

Boundary #3 – Meet with your pastor or accountability partner on a regular basis for reports and support.

You will meet once a week with your pastor, ministry leader and/or accountability partner(s) to discuss progress, report on challenges, and receive prayer and encouragement.

Our Motivation: To know that you are here for the purpose of growing spiritually and creating healthy accountable relationships.

Boundary #4 – Church Designated Leader

Yosemite Church will designate a leader to observe your behavior, to come alongside you, to support your growth, and to ensure that the requirements stated here are being honored. If the requirements are not being honored, we will ask you not to attend or participate in church activities, ministries and weekend services.

Our Motivation: To know that you are taking our concerns seriously and that you are focusing on making healthy choices and building trust with those to whom you are accountable.

Designated Leader(s): _____

_____

Name of individual: _____

Address: _____

Home Phone: _____ Cell Phone: _____

E-mail Address: _____

Date: _____ Date of next review: _____

Garage Gyms

Several years ago as a way to spend more intentional time with some of the guys that I was investing in (Mentoring and discipling), we began to exercise together. This progressed from running to purchasing a couple of TRX exercise straps. These very versatile devices are intended to strengthen the body's core along with every appendage. I mounted 4-5 hooks in the ceiling of my garage. Before I knew it, 5-6 guys were coming four days a week to exercise both their bodies and their spirits in my garage. More guys expressed interest so I put up 6 more hooks expanding out under the eaves of the house. Because I had a large cement section beside my house, an 18-foot bar was added where I could squeeze in another five guys. What was good for a couple of guys, a place to exercise and practice our faith daily with others, seemed to strike a chord with more and more men. It wasn't long before there were a consistent group of 10-12 guys that could morph to 15 any morning. One gym turned into two, and then three and now they continue to grow as a way to strengthen not just the physical but the spiritual lives of men and now women, too.

How are the gyms organized? Each gym follows the same set of practices. We call it our Garage gym DNA.

1. First, every participant coming gets a hug first thing, even if late. Physical affection and affirmation are an important parts of our spiritual community. They are power and simple ways to acknowledge one another and affirm each other's presence.

2. Right on time, we all huddle arms around one another's shoulders and someone opens in prayer.

3. Then the TRX routine begins. There are many well-designed exercise routines to choose from. Someone in the group might have a greater passion to put this together. The actual exercise will take close to an hour. Working out four days a week allows for a good rotation of arm and legs.

4. After the set, our TRX routine is complete everyone grabs their yoga mat and forms a circle. As we go through some floor stretching, someone will begin one of several spiritual prayer disciplines – gratitude, confession, dieing to self or intercession. Usually we'll offer gratitude prayers every time and throw one of the others in on occasion. When these practices are done daily, they cannot help but change the way we see life, people, God and the struggles we face each day.

GROWTH

Get to know them better
Reach for their heart
Open the Bible with them
Work on their goals with them
Take time to pray with them
Hold them accountable

Managing Your
Mouth Survey

(You as evaluated by someone else.)

Take a quick survey to see if this is an area of strength of weakness.
1= No or Rarely   3=Sometimes   5=Yes or Frequently

1. I complain about others.   1 2 3 4 5

2. I have complimented someone today.   1 2 3 4 5

3. I have recently participated in gossip   1 2 3 4 5
 (spoken negatively about others).

4. I look for ways to encourage others up with my words. 1 2 3 4 5

5. I exaggerate when I tell a story.   1 2 3 4 5

6. I have expressed gratitude to someone today.   1 2 3 4 5

7. I have been told I talk too much.   1 2 3 4 5

8. I have excused myself from a   1 2 3 4 5
 conversation of gossip.

9. I rationalize why I'm not completely honest.   1 2 3 4 5

10. I have expressed thankfulness to God today.   1 2 3 4 5

11. I speak my assumptions before   1 2 3 4 5
 checking the facts.

12. I think about the impact of my words   1 2 3 4 5
 before I speak.

Now, add up your score for the even numbered statements and record it below, and then add up your score for the odd numbered statements.

Even Number Score _____   Odd Number Score _____

From 21-30	This is an area of strength	From 6-13
From 14-20	This needs improvement	From 14-20
From 6-13	Improvement is critical	From 21-30

YC Membership Commitment

Name _____ Date of Birth _____

Please transfer each of your survey answers on the lines below:

Family Role: _____

What you are good at doing: _____

Connect Survey Answer: _____

Grow Survey Answer: _____

Serve Survey Answers:

1. _____

2. _____

3. _____

I would like to take the following next steps:

_____ Get baptized:
_____ Take the baptism class
_____ Join a group
_____ Serve on a team
_____ Schedule me to meet with a ministry leader
_____ May we text you? If yes, cell number: _____
_____ I would like to speak with a pastor

I have made a commitment to Christ.   Yes   No

I have been baptized as an adult.   Yes   No

Do you affirm the Mission, Vision and Values of Yosemite Church?
Yes   No

Are you committed to making the vision a reality by pursuing it in your own life?   Yes   No

Are you committing to pursue a daily time with Christ and to connect with God, grow in community and serve God's purposes at Yosemite Church?   Yes   No

What time of the day was best for you to meet with Christ?

Morning   Noon   Night

I would like to become a member of Yosemite Church.

_____ / _____
Signature/ Date

Current Ministry Involvement: _____

_____

_____

Call to schedule an interview

Parachurches

Alpha Pregnancy Center
www.alphaphc.com

Celebration Radio 101.5 KAMB
www.celebrationradio.com

Habitat For Humanity
www.hfhmerced.org

Love INC
www.loveincmerced.com

Love Merced
www.lovemerced.com

Mary's Mantle
www.jmjmaternityhome.org

Merced County Food Bank
www.mercedcountyfoodbank.org

Merced County Jail Ministry
Email: jespreach01@att.net

Merced County Rescue Mission
www.mercedrescuemission.org

The Salvation Army
www.tsagoldenstate.org/goldenstate/Merced_Corps

Young Life
www.mercedcounty.younglife.org

Key Area Work List

Week Beginning: _____

1. _____
   ___ _____
   ___ _____
   ___ _____
   ___ _____

2. _____
   ___ _____
   ___ _____
   ___ _____
   ___ _____

3. _____
   ___ _____
   ___ _____
   ___ _____
   ___ _____

4. _____
   ___ _____
   ___ _____
   ___ _____
   ___ _____

5. _____
   ___ _____
   ___ _____
   ___ _____
   ___ _____

6. _____
   ___ _____
   ___ _____
   ___ _____
   ___ _____

7. _____
   ___ _____
   ___ _____
   ___ _____

	Monday	Tuesday	Wednesday	Thursday	Friday	Saturday	Sunday
5am							
6am							
7am							
8am							
9am							
10am							
11am							
12pm							
1pm							
2pm							
3pm							
4pm							
5pm							
6pm							
7pm							
8pm							
9pm							

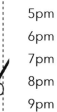

Key Area Work List

Week Beginning: _____

1. _____

   ___ _____
   ___ _____
   ___ _____

2. _____

   ___ _____
   ___ _____
   ___ _____

3. _____

   ___ _____
   ___ _____
   ___ _____

4. _____

   ___ _____
   ___ _____
   ___ _____

5. _____

   ___ _____
   ___ _____
   ___ _____

6. _____

   ___ _____
   ___ _____
   ___ _____

7. _____

   ___ _____
   ___ _____
   ___ _____

	Monday	Tuesday	Wednesday	Thursday	Friday	Saturday	Sunday
5am							
6am							
7am							
8am							
9am							
10am							
11am							
12pm							
1pm							
2pm							
3pm							
4pm							
5pm							
6pm							
7pm							
8pm							
9pm							

My Spiritual Growth Plan

CONNECT

Prayer & Bible Engagement: When/Where: Accountability:

GROW

Who: When: Where: Our Disciplines:

SERVE

To be equipped to serve: I will serve by:

SELF AWARENESS

Potential Goals:

My Spiritual Growth Plan

CONNECT

Prayer & Bible Engagement: When/Where: Accountability:

GROW

Who: When: Where: Our Disciplines:

SERVE

To be equipped to serve: I will serve by:

SELF AWARENESS

Potential Goals:

My Spiritual Growth Plan

CONNECT

Prayer & Bible Engagement:

When/Where:

Accountability:

GROW

Who:

When:

Where:

Our Disciplines:

SERVE

To be equipped to serve:

I will serve by:

SELF AWARENESS

Potential Goals:

35619568R00151

Made in the USA
San Bernardino, CA
30 June 2016